It was only a matter of time before a clever publisher realized that there is an audience for whom *Exile on Main Street* or *Electric Ladyland* are as significant and worthy of study as *The Catcher in the Rye* or *Middlemarch* … The series … is freewheeling and eclectic, ranging from minute rock-geek analysis to idiosyncratic personal celebration — *The New York Times Book Review*

Ideal for the rock geek who thinks liner notes just aren't enough — *Rolling Stone*

One of the coolest publishing imprints on the planet — *Bookslut*

These are for the insane collectors out there who appreciate fantastic design, well-executed thinking, and things that make your house look cool. Each volume in this series takes a seminal album and breaks it down in startling minutiae. We love these. We are huge nerds — *Vice*

A brilliant series … each one a work of real love — *NME* (UK)

Passionate, obsessive, and smart — *Nylon*

Religious tracts for the rock 'n' roll faithful — *Boldtype*

[A] consistently excellent series — *Uncut* (UK)

We … aren't naive enough to think that we're your only source for reading about music (but if we had our way … watch out). For those of you who really like to know everything there is to know about an album, you'd do well to check out Continuum's "33 1/3" series of books — *Pitchfork*

For reviews of individual titles in the series, please visit our blog at 333sound.com and our website at http://www.bloomsbury.com/musicandsoundstudies

Follow us on Twitter: @333books

Like us on Facebook: https://www.facebook.com/33.3books

For a complete list of books in this series, see the back of this book

For more information about the series, please visit our new blog:

www.333sound.com

Where you'll find:

– Author and artist interviews

– Author profiles

– News about the series

– How to submit a proposal to our open call

– Things we find amusing

Let It Be

Colin Meloy

BLOOMSBURY ACADEMIC
NEW YORK • LONDON • OXFORD • NEW DELHI • SYDNEY

BLOOMSBURY ACADEMIC
Bloomsbury Publishing Inc
1385 Broadway, New York, NY 10018, USA
50 Bedford Square, London, WC1B 3DP, UK
29 Earlsfort Terrace, Dublin 2, Ireland

BLOOMSBURY, BLOOMSBURY ACADEMIC and the Diana logo are trademarks
of Bloomsbury Publishing Plc

First published in 2004 by the Continuum International Publishing Group Inc
Reprinted 2011
Reprinted by Bloomsbury Academic 2013, 2014, 2016, 2019, 2020 (twice), 2021,
2022, 2023 (twice), 2024

Meloy, Colin
Let it be/Colin Meloy
p. cm. — (33 1/3)
ISBN 0-8264-1633-0 (pbk. : alk. paper)
1. Replacements (Musical group). Let it be. 2. Meloy, Colin,
I. Title. II. Series.
ML421.R47M45 2004
782.42166'092'2–dc22
2004009561

ISBN: PB: 978-0-8264-1633-9
ePDF: 978-1-4411-3825-5
ePub: 978-1-4411-9448-0

Series: 33 1/3, volume 16

Printed and bound in Great Britain

To find out more about our authors and books visit www.bloomsbury.com
and sign up for our newsletters.

Foreword

I would consider myself an avid music listener. I own a lot of records; the bands and records that have changed and influenced both my life and the music that I write are innumerable, so when I was approached to contribute a volume to the 33 1/3 series, I was a bit stumped as to what to pick. One definitive record that, above all else, could be considered my favorite record of all time. After a moderate amount of deliberation, I managed to pare my standard top ten (a list, I discovered, that has remained for the most part unchanged since I was eighteen years old) down to a few monumental, groundbreaking records. Naturally, the Replacements' *Let It Be* was among these finalists. For varying reasons, it won out over a Robyn Hitchcock record and a Smiths record, though I maintain that once you get up into the top tiers of one's list of favorite records, there is little that distinguishes one record from being better or more favored than the others. My choice came as a surprise to most people to whom I described the project—mostly, I imagine, because the music I play is not particularly Replacements-esque. These deceptive appearances aside, I cannot stress enough what an influence the entire oeuvre of the 'Mats has been on me as a person and a musician. In the following pages, I have attempted to spell that out as best I can.

The music that I write strays on the side of the fantastic, so I will say that it was not an inconsiderable challenge to tarry so long in the realm of the non-fictive. I have the following people to thank for my eventual survival in this endeavor: my kind, patient, benevolent and lovely girlfriend and co-conspirator Carson Ellis, my sister Maile, Paul Montagne, my remarkable and patient bandmates for forgiving me the time I took to write this, and my editor in this project, David Barker.

March 14, 2004
Childress, Texas

I stood on the corner of State and Rodney in my Keds and Levis, hands stuffed in the pocket of my hooded sweatshirt, waiting for Mark. I could see him a ways off, kicking along the sidewalk. I was impatient and shouted for him to hurry up. In my sweatshirt pocket I could feel the ten-dollar bill I had earned from mowing lawns that spring, and I crumpled and uncrumpled it between my fingers while I waited. It was 1987; we had just graduated from elementary school and were gearing up for the plunge into the middle school.

"Ready?" I asked when he got to the corner.

"Yep," he said.

We walked down Rodney, past the old Governor's mansion, past the May Butler school where my mother had worked for a short time, teaching life science to high school dropouts, when it was the Project for Alternative Living. We shuffled down past the Red Meadow and Jester's Bar, their sidewalk curbs all fender to fender with Harley Davidson motorcycles. We talked about school, about the girls we would meet at our new school. Mark had had more experience with girls than I had and he talked about dating, how you're not supposed to talk about school on a date.

"It'll just make 'em bored," he said.

"Really?" I said. I was imagining myself on a date with a girl: we were sitting at a booth at the Parrot confectionary; she toyed with her sundae straw while I yammered on about my English homework. I tried several times to revise the fantasy in my mind, but I couldn't get the me in the fantasy to talk about anything but school. I was doomed.

We were walking to Pegasus Music at the mall, that day, to buy a cassette. Actually, I was the one buying the cassette; Mark was just along for the walk. It was a Saturday and we both had little else to do.

The air was crisp and there were melting remnants of snow on the edges of the sidewalks—the glacial core of a drift that had fallen in February, now seeing its final demise in April. Veins of mud ran across the surface of the snow.

At the time, there were two record stores of note in Helena, Montana, where I was born. One was Pegasus Music, where Mark and I were walking that afternoon, and the other was Henry J's. Henry J's was on the west side of town, on Euclid, past Ben Franklin's. It was owned by two guys in their forties. The clerks wore mustaches and bandannas and they played the Rolling Stones over the in-store stereo. My dad bought records there because it was on the way to our house in the valley and I often went in with him. I remember someone buying a Prudence Dredge record there, the one with the cartoon cover, and I overheard the clerk highly recommending it to the purchaser. The first two records I ever owned came from Henry J's. They were *Chicago 16* and *Cargo* by Men at Work and my mother had bought them for me for my birthday. I had heard each of the records' respective singles on the radio and had asked for the albums by name, along with my usual list of the year's latest *Star Wars* toys. It was seen as a sign of my maturation.

We walked past St. Helena's Cathedral, with its stained glass windows and spires, and I told Mark about how I'd heard that someone, back in the old days, had flown a plane between the two spires to win a bet. We both stopped for a moment and stared up a the spires, at the golden crosses atop each spire and imagined a bi-plane speeding, wheeling, through the space between them, its goggled pilot still drunk from the night before.

"Really?" asked Mark.

"Yep," I said, and we kept walking.

We turned right on Neill Avenue, walking carefully over the weather-wracked sidewalks, the cement all cracked and upended by another harsh winter. Crossing Montana Avenue, we stopped momentarily at the Mini Mart for Sweet-Tarts and taffy. In the corner of the store there was a video game called Shenobi where for twenty-five cents you assumed the role of a martial artist in your choice of red or white robes, fighting for the love of a short, digitized geisha who expressed her love for the winner in pixilated hearts that appeared above her head. With the change Mark had in his pocket, we played a few games; he played the white-robe fighter, I was the red-robed. When neither of us succeeded in winning the affections of the geisha, we shrugged our shoulders, pocketed our candy and continued on our walk to Pegasus Music.

The last few blocks to the Capitol Hill Mall were quick and the scenery was bland. Neill Avenue past Montana Avenue was just a series of strip malls and office buildings. The mall parking lot was full, this being a Saturday, and we zigzagged between parked cars to reach the entrance through the J. C. Penney's on the west side. We followed the granite tiles in the floor that made a trail through the clothing racks and perfume counters of the department store, to the place where Penney's gave way to the mall's main corridor. There was only one corridor in this mall and it ran east to west in a straight, continuous line.

We were hungry but I wanted to go to Pegasus Music first. We didn't know if we'd have money left over for Bob's Pizza, where the food sat under brilliant red lights on the counter top and the counter girls were beautiful and bitter and mean. We could see Pegasus Music from yards away; the neon above its entryway cast bright blue and pink reflections across the polished mall floor. There was a horse with wings in white neon galloping along the pink and blue rainbow above the doorway. Inside, everything was brilliantly white. We walked along the rows of racks of tapes that covered the walls, gliding our fingers along the spines of the cassettes. A boy sat behind the cash register, silently flipping through a magazine. He looked up briefly to watch the two of us entering the store, and then looked back at the pages.

Mark wandered off to the two rows of compact disc bins that sat in the middle of the room and began shuffling through the CDs in their long, colorful boxes and shoplifter-proof plastic sheaves. I walked to the R's. There was a poster over the tape racks advertising the Jesus and Mary Chain's *Darklands*, and I stopped and marveled at their black hair and their black sunglasses. I decided I wanted hair like the Jesus and Mary Chain's. I wanted black hair and black sunglasses. Hair that sprouted from my head like a geyser. I wondered how they got it to stay up like that.

In the R's, I traced my fingers over the spines of the cassettes until I got to the Replacements. There were two of them: *Pleased to Meet Me* and *Let It Be*. With a little difficulty, I slid both of them from their space on the rack, letting three R.E.O. Speedwagon tapes fall down into their place. I scanned the song listing on both of them, turned them over, and studied the covers, side by side. On one were two hands shaking, on the other were four guys sitting on a rooftop. I squinted at this one, studying each of the characters individually: one was mop-topped and looked like he was rubbing something out of his eye; one had black curly hair and was looking away from the camera, like he didn't know that the picture was being taken; there was a blond haired one behind him who was smirking; and one guy in the back with unruly black hair, craning his neck over the other three to make good for the camera. I slid *Pleased to Meet Me* back into the rack above the R.E.O. Speedwagon tapes and walked to the cash register, *Let It Be* in hand. Mark saw that I was ready and put away a CD he had been looking at.

The boy at the cash register looked up from his magazine and took the tape from my hand. He took my ten-dollar bill and gave me a couple bucks in change. He slammed the tape into a machine that removed the security sheaf and handed the naked, cellophaned cassette to me. "Have a good day," he said, halfheartedly, and returned to his magazine. Mark and I smiled at each other.

We shared a piece of pepperoni pizza from Bob's Pizza and talked about the counter girls.

We walked home in silence and I absently swung the plastic bag with the tape in it back and forth. We took a different route back; we headed up Montana Ave., past the Capitol building. There was a soccer practice in session and a crowd of kids decked out in YMCA t-shirts ran at each other wildly while their coach paced the distance between two orange cones, barking drilling instructions. We turned right on Broadway, down past Jefferson School and took the short cut on the lee side of Sugarloaf Hill to make it to my mother's house. The house was empty when we arrived and we helped ourselves to the granola bars in the pantry.

"Let's listen to it," Mark said, between mouthfuls.

I wrestled the tape from the cellophane and put it in my mother's tape deck. From the speakers came a breath and then the first chords struck. The song was called "I Will Dare," and Mark and I stared at each other in rapt attention. I had heard the song before; my uncle had sent it to me on a tape that Christmas. The next song, "Favorite Thing," had us nodding our heads to the beat. By the third song, with its frenetic *bum-chick* drumbeat, we were jumping around the room, trying to do our best imitation of slam dancing. We tripped and laughed and caught ourselves, trying not to destroy any of the pottery that sat on the side tables of my mother's living room. The song dipped into a sort of jazz break down and we stopped to catch our breaths. Then the next song came on and we were back at it, but this time we were throwing each other around the room and we were shouting too. The song was about someone named Tommy getting his tonsils out. The chorus went "Rip, rip, we're gonna rip 'em out now!"

We ran into the pantry and grabbed a can of red spray paint and sprinted out into the yard where we found a dejected plastic sled, leaning up against the fence. Howling, we spray painted "PUNK ROCK!" all over it.

*   *   *

Mark was blond haired, blue eyed, broad nosed and pretty tall for his age; when we played *Star Wars*, I was always Han Solo to his Luke Skywalker. We grew up right across from each other at the end of South Rodney Street in Helena, on top of a hill called the Rodney Hill. There were two ways to our houses: the straight way and the crooked way. The crooked way ran a rough half-mile along the west side of the hill on a windy dirt road. The straight way went straight up the steep incline of the Rodney hill and in the winter would be covered with an impassable sheen of ice. The straight way was a deathtrap for the unprepared driver; the only way to attempt this passage was to gun it from five blocks out and try to make the entire hill without slipping. If you started slipping, you were doomed. More than a few people attempted the straight way in the dead of winter only to spin a 360 halfway up, and slide back down. If the snow was bad, the crooked way, with its small hills and blind corners, would be impassable until it was plowed and your only choice would be to brave the straight way. The more faint of heart would park their cars at the bottom of the hill and march up the hill on foot. The straight way proved a brilliant sledding track and in the 70s, on a particularly wintry day, some friends of my parents sledded the entire distance from the top of the hill to the public library, a mile away, on the back of a wooden Radio Flyer.

Our parents had been friends for longer than we had been alive and Mark's mother often told me about how she would baby-sit me when I was a baby and Mark was still in her belly. She would lay me over her belly and I would fall asleep and Mark, who was normally very active in the womb, would stop kicking for a bit and would fall asleep as well. Mark lived in a brown shingled house with a big yard and a basement that smelled like cat pee and mildew.

When we were very young we liked to mug for photographs by hugging each other fiercely, with our noses all scrunched and our eyes pursed shut and our cheeks pressed tightly together. We would do it at the slightest provocation—as soon as an adult would bring out a camera, we were there, our arms wound so tightly around the other's torso that we struggled to catch our breaths. Mark always had a drip of snot running from his nose to his upper lip. In second grade, Mark's mother moved to New Zealand and took Mark with her and I was deprived of my best friend for six months. At the after-school daycare that we both went to, I was quiet and removed and didn't speak to anyone. When he got back, most of the second grade year had passed. He called my house from across the street.

"I'm home!" he said.

We ran out of our houses to meet each other in the middle of the gravel road. We stopped short of embracing each other and looked at each other, puzzled.

"You don't have snot on your nose," I said.

From that point on, we never hugged each other like we had before he left for New Zealand, even when the adults with their cameras asked us to.

Our houses on top of the Rodney Hill marked the southern end of the Helena city limits and looked out on an expanse of private property and National Park land that stretched for miles behind our houses. In the gullies and washes surrounding the Rodney Hill there was a variety of man-made caves, each varying in the length and depth. We gave names to each of them. There was Indian Cave, in which we imagined there were ancient cave drawings and which was so long that it took several intrepid visits before we mustered the courage to make it to the end; Lunch Cave was the smallest of them, a divot in the earth, and was closest to our houses—we would carry our peanut butter and jelly sandwiches there and eat them as a resting point between caves; below that was Sleep Cave, which was sinister and deep and had a dirty, deteriorating mattress at the very end of it with rusted tin cans scattered around it. We drew maps of the area around our houses; we dreamed of setting up an amusement park where we would lead guided tours through the different caves we had discovered.

Our parents rarely put any boundaries on our playing—that we not watch TV during the day was really the only overriding stricture we were forced to follow. We were never castigated for crawling around in what were essentially abandoned mine shafts, obviously inhabited by homeless vagabonds. When we regaled our parents with our discoveries (the pocket knife we found in Indian Cave, the tattered suit coat we found in Sleep Cave) they only smiled and quietly supported our explorations.

By the time Mark returned from New Zealand, our families had begun to unravel. Our parents had met and had children around the same time and they divorced simultaneously, too. I sat in the back of my mother's car as we drove away from the Rodney Hill house. My father was helping her move back into the house where they had lived when I was born, and I watched her green-plated stereo receiver, strapped tight to a sofa cushion on the bed of my father's truck, recede into the distance as we followed the truck down the straight way.

My father stayed on at the Rodney Hill house for five years after that, and while I spent half of the year at my mother's house in town, I still spent as much time as I could with Mark. His mother had moved out of the brown-shingled house into an outbuilding that his father had built a few yards from the house. Mark told me it was a bathhouse—it had a sauna in it—and its completion happened to coincide with his parents' divorce. As it happened, there was plenty of room for a bed and a kitchen.

Our explorations of the Rodney Hill and its environs began to extend farther and farther away from our houses. A mile's walk south of our houses, via a rough snowmobile track, led to a meadow in the middle of a large stand of trees. The meadow was as far as we were willing to go away from the safety of home; farther south, the meadow turned back to trees and the landscape disappeared over a small ridge. We were both ten years old when we decided to organize an adult-free overnight backpacking expedition to the meadow.

We prepared in Mark's basement, pulling backpacks and kitchen gear from the closet below the staircase. We wore thick wool pants and packed extra pairs of wool socks. We brought cans of Van DeCamp's Pork and Beans and instant oatmeal and Top Ramen. We packed plates and bowls and two full sets of kitchen utensils. We stuffed the backpack side pockets with bags of Gummi worms and cans of Pepsi. We tried to fit the Coleman stove into Mark's green external pack, but it wouldn't fit so we resolved to carry it. We grabbed a two-gallon container from the storage shed and filled it with water. By the time we were ready to go, we could scarcely walk fifty feet without having to stop to rest.

"Ready?" Mark asked, adjusting the straps on my pack. He slapped the sides a few times for dramatic effect. The Pepsi sloshed in its cans.

"Yeah," I said, and turned around to do the same to Mark's pack. There was a Rolling Stones patch on the back of it, its big red tongue lolling. I jostled the pockets and yanked on some straps. "Good to go," I said.

We traded off carrying the metal green Coleman stove and the two gallons of water. We stopped to rest often as we followed the trail to the meadow. We stopped at the top of the first hill, the one that we used as a toboggan hill in the winter, where we could still see the roofs of our houses and the rooftops and buildings of the city in the valley. We stopped where the snowmobile road split in two; the right fork led down into the gulch and to Unionville, where my friend Matt lived with his divorced hippie father in a big white teepee. We stopped at another fork in the road, where the dual tracks of the road split into two single track trails and one trail led up onto a ridge and the other stayed low. We followed the low path to save our backs and knees; we broke into the bag of Gummi worms and ate some of them, sucking them through puckered lips and rolling them between our cheeks and our gums. We ventured guesses about the weight of our packs. Mark had been on more backpacking trips than I, and his guesses always trumped mine. When we finally arrived at the meadow, it was late evening and we immediately unpacked and set up our camp. We erected the tent that we'd borrowed from our parents, its size ample for our two small bodies, and cobbled together a space to be our kitchen. We tried to start the Coleman stove, but couldn't. We pumped at the little gas tank as much as our arms could manage, but each time we set a match to the burner, nothing happened. Eventually, we gave up and cursed the green metal stove and kicked ourselves for bringing such a useless piece of dead weight.

"We'll just eat stuff that we don't have to cook," offered Mark, looking at our packs despondently.

I nodded, though I couldn't remember packing anything that didn't require cooking. A brief search through our packs confirmed my suspicion and we sat down to a dinner of leftover Gummi worms and Pepsi. We were tempted to walk back home, but it was getting dark and the journey seemed much too daunting in the dark. We crawled into our sleeping bags in our big domed tent and finished the rest of the Gummi worms. The soda gurgled in our empty stomachs and I pulled out my dad's worn Modern Library collection of Victorian ghost stories and began reading. It was a story about two men in Hungary, canoeing on a flooded branch of the Danube through an inhospitable landscape. I got to the part where the two men were camped on a small sand bar, where the water was lapping closer to their tent and the willows that surrounded them were beginning to appear to move closer, when I heard Mark softly crying.

"Are you okay?" I asked, closing the book on my thumb.

"Yeah," he said, sniffing away the tears, "I'm just kinda hungry, I guess."

Outside the wind whipped against the tent wall and the sound of revving truck engines echoed in the gulch below the meadow. Mark started crying again and I put the book away and started hugging him. We both lay in the dark, listening to the night sounds, with our arms out of our sleeping bags and wrapped tightly around each other like we used to do when we mugged for photographs.

We woke up with the sun shining through the tent mesh and Mark, now desperately hungry, poured cold water over a bowl of instant oatmeal and ate it, grimacing. There were packages of Top Ramen torn open and strewn about the campsite, remnants of some raccoon's midnight snack. We silently packed up our tent and sleeping bags and half-heartedly stuffed it all into our backpacks. Trudging back home from the meadow, Mark said, "Don't tell anyone that I cried, okay?"

"Okay," I said. When we told the story over dinner at Mark's house a week later and we all laughed so hard that Mark's dad started tearing up, I didn't mention that Mark had cried and I had hugged him until we both had fallen asleep.

*   *   *

Like every other kid that lived on the Rodney Hill, Mark and I went to school at Central Elementary. It was a long brick building, across the street from the Cathedral. On cold days when I walked from my mom's house on Ewing Street, I would cut through the Cathedral, walking silently on the plush red carpets under the massive vaulted ceilings and frescoed porticos. I brought *Star Wars* figures in my backpack and would walk them along the arms of the pews, jumping them from pew to pew, whispering the noise of the jet packs that allowed them to fly. When we were in third grade, Mark's mother moved out of the bathhouse on the Rodney Hill and into an apartment near Central School. We would meet there every day before school and walk the remaining few blocks together. Her apartment was small, the upstairs floor of a house, and had only one bedroom. Mark's room was a walk-in closet and there was barely room for his small twin bed and a bedside table. He liked it though; he said he felt like an orphan.

Mark was handsome and athletic; he played basketball and football at school. I was relatively well known in my school for an off-kilter imagination that had inspired the two plays I had written and produced in second and third grade: *The Bloody Knight* and its sequel, *The Bloody Knight Two*. My classmates all jockeyed for prominent parts in these plays; I reveled in the attention, not knowing that popularity on account of a wild imagination was a fleeting thing.

*   *   *

Tygen's mother had lived in New York and her apartment was covered in trappings of the city: posters of Manhattan adorned the walls, and the coffee tables and lamps were covered with dark purple batik cloths. When she spoke, her consonants were rounded by a soft, vaguely east coast accent. She rented the apartment from our family's friends, the Hatches, who lived downstairs in the massive Victorian house on Rodney, near the middle school. She was one of three employees at the local art cinema and she smoked cigarettes occasionally. She too had divorced from her husband around the time of my parents' divorce and her ex-husband had moved to Noxon, a remote town in northwest Montana, where Tygen said everybody grew pot and there were crazy rednecks in the woods who had sex with their daughters. Tygen referred to his father by his first name, not by "dad" like the rest of us.

Tygen's mother's living room was filled with records. Tygen and I sat on the floor and thumbed through them. Present were the Paul Simon and Joni Mitchell records that filled the shelves of my own mother's record collection, but there were many that I didn't recognize. Elvis Costello. The Velvet Underground. Blondie. Their covers were stark and strangely violent.

* * *

My mother didn't have a television, and it was an embarrassment. Not that she couldn't afford one; she deliberately decided we should live without one. When the other kids in my class talked about *Taxi* and *Little House on the Prairie*, I had to feign knowledge of the programs. My father had a TV at our house on the Rodney Hill, but we didn't have cable. We did, however, have HBO via a small brown box that sat below the television set. But because we were not allowed to watch TV during the day, we were limited to what movies or programs were played between the hours immediately after dusk and our bedtime. What we were allowed to watch, however, was real prime stuff. While my father might have been proprietary about the times when we watched TV, he had little compunction about what we watched. I distinctly recall watching *The Shining* at a very young age, my sister and I hunkered down in front of the television, our eyes wide as young Danny raced his Big Wheel through the labyrinthine hallways of the Overlook Hotel. When the sexed-up Kathleen Turner/John Hurt thriller *Body Heat* played on HBO, my dad recommended it to us, explaining how much we would like it, if it weren't so dirty.

Mark's father, in the brown-shingled house, had cable. We would sit in the basement den and watch television, Mark opting for daytime re-runs of *Dukes of Hazzard* while I angled for MTV.

Like most kids of my generation, I first discovered MTV as an advertisement—I sat in my grandparents' living room, placidly watching a baseball game with my grandfather, when a dayglo-spattered commercial segment flashed across the screen, concluding with a sunglassed and mohawked man pointing an extended finger at the screen—at my grandfather and I—and shouting "I WANT MY MTV!" Shocked, I looked over at my grandfather. He didn't seem to register it. It would be years before the cable channel became its ubiquitous, generation-defining self, but this image was seared in my brain. My grandparents eventually did get MTV, though I imagine they had little choice in the matter. It was entertaining, however, to imagine my grandfather getting on the phone with their cable operator and shouting "I WANT MY MTV!" into the receiver. But most of my MTV-watching was done in the confines of Mark's basement, sitting on a ratty couch and drinking Pepsi even though Mark didn't really care for MTV.

For his tenth birthday, Mark got a muscle t-shirt with an Asian dragon silk-screened in gold across the chest. I immediately envied him for it and we took turns putting it on and practicing our air-guitar riffs while jumping around his living room. We decided then that we should start a band. I insisted on being the lead singer. Mark quietly agreed and became the guitar player. We decided that the name of our band would be the Babies and, lacking instruments, we would perform our songs on brooms and laundry baskets. We enlisted the help of two of our friends, Spencer and Ben, to fill out the lineup. I suggested that our songs be parodies of current hit songs, knowing full well that the writing process would require hours spent watching MTV. Mark quietly consented.

Every summer in August, grasshoppers would take over the yards and gardens of Helena homes, a blight that was practically of biblical proportions. The grass was yellow and brittle at that time of year, parched from another dry summer, making our footsteps crackle when we played on the lawn. The grasshoppers blanketed the yellow grass and would scatter wildly when we ran over them, adhering to our calves and bouncing off of our shirt sleeves. Mark's parents organized a party one year, calling it Hopper Daze, and suggested that the party-goers find a suitable grasshopper to enter and perform in a number of competitions. A series of wood blocks constituted an obstacle course; a long, thin plywood box served as a racing track. There were beauty contests held (Mark and I boiled ours one year, turning the grasshopper's carapace a deep, crimson red—a sure winner until we were disqualified for having killed our entrant), and competitions to see who could hold a live grasshopper in their mouth the longest. Mark and I decided that this party would be the perfect time to debut our rock band. We organized our side players and jotted down ideas for potential songs. On my insistence, we watched a lot of MTV. We made up new words to Bruce Springsteen's "Glory Days," and to Cheap Trick's "Surrender." We changed Prince's "Raspberry Beret" to "Blueberry French Hat," and marveled at our cleverness:

Blueberry French hat
The kind that you find in the toy section
Blueberry French hat
I wanna buuuuy it.

August rolled around and the grasshoppers began to wreak havoc on the turnips and cabbages of the Rodney Hill gardens while Mark and I geared up for our big debut. My mother bought me a matching Chinese Dragon muscle shirt, this one in white with red screen printing, and Mark and I picked out the best brooms from his dad's utility closet. I picked the long handled broom, one that would work best as a microphone stand and Mark chose the one with the largest bristles, that most resembled an electric guitar.

We performed to roughly two dozen adults, all standing agog as we jumped around on our homemade stage, scissor kicking and pumping our fists. We screamed our lyrics, rendering them unintelligible—except one line, which my mother still remembers. For our rendition of Cheap Trick's "Surrender," we chose to keep the main lyric intact: "Mommy's all right / Daddy's all right / They just seem a little weird." She glanced over at Mark's mother, who was, like my mom, in the midst of finalizing her divorce. They caught each other's eyes, smiled, and shrugged their shoulders. The set ran roughly six songs and we were done, walking off stage, waving at the cheering crowd. Spencer threw his birch tree drum sticks into the audience, only to see one of the neighborhood dogs pick them up and run off. We were thrilled with the performance. We talked about our next show (we called it a gig), about what songs we would perform, and how we would save up for instruments; there was a pawn shop on Rodney, across the street from the Red Meadow Bar, and electric guitars hung like bats across the storefront window.

"We'll watch more MTV," I suggested to Mark, "And we'll learn more songs!"

Mark grumbled something about needing to spend more time outside.

*   *   *

My uncle Paul came to Helena in the summer of 1983. He was the youngest of my mom's siblings—my mother was fifteen when he was born—but they seemed to be the most aligned of the whole family. He was twenty years old, in his third year at the University of Oregon.

"Hi, kiddo," he said as he climbed out of the car.

The last time I had seen Paul had been at my aunt's house during Christmas break a year prior. It had been uncommonly cold; the pool had frozen over and my uncle and my cousin Matthew had spent the better part of a day breaking the ice in the chlorine blue water.

Matthew was six years older than I was and he and Paul had slept in the same room where they stayed in bed until noon. I sat on the enormous leather couch and played Frogger on my watch, waiting for them to wake up. When they finally rose, I would follow them from room to room, sitting quietly as they shot pool in the garage, nodding understandingly while they discussed the finer qualities of the Police's *Zenyatta Mondatta*. But now he was traveling back to school and was stopping in Montana to see his sister and his niece and nephew. He had timed his trip to coincide with a few Grateful Dead concerts that were happening on the west coast.

I offered to carry his luggage into the house. "How long are you staying?" I asked.

"A few days," he said, "I have to be in Seattle on Tuesday. The Dead are playing at the arena."

"Okay," I said, confused.

"Here," he said, "Help me carry this." He led me around to the trunk of the car and, popping the hatch, he handed me a heavy guitar case. There were stickers from various Eugene record stores pasted over the torn black exterior.

"Is this your guitar?" I asked.

"What do you think it is? A machine gun?" he asked, straight faced. He grabbed a faded blue duffel out of the car, slammed the hatch and walked towards the house. I followed unsteadily, my small arms wrapped around the guitar case as if I was holding it in a headlock. Every few steps, the bottom would drag on the ground and I would stop to reposition it in my arms.

My mother was waiting at the door. "Hi Paul," she said.

"Hi, sis," he replied. They hugged in the doorway and I stood behind Paul, resting my burden on the ground as I stopped to catch my breath.

That night after dinner, we sat in the living room talking. Mom made a pot of decaf for she and Paul; my sister and I ate ice cream and sat cross legged on the living room floor, listening to their conversation. They talked about their parents and Paul's classes at the University of Oregon; Paul asked after my dad and my mom shrugged, saying she hadn't talked to him in a few months. When they finished their coffee, my mom asked if Paul would like a beer.

"Sure," he said.

After a while, at my mother's urging, Paul got up and opened the guitar case. It was a twelve string Alvarez and its headstock was lanky on the neck. He took a few moments to tune, took a sip from his beer, and began playing "The Needle and the Damage Done." My mom smiled and tapped her foot, singing along to the "gone, gone, the damage done," parts. When he finished we applauded. He asked my sister and I if we had any requests.

"Can you play a song by the Ernie Nernie Nert Band?" I asked, stumbling over my question.

"The what?"

"He means the Nitty Gritty Dirt Band," my mother explained.

"Oh," said Paul, "I don't think so." He turned to my sister, "What about you?"

"Prince, maybe?" she asked.

"How can you guys listen to that crap?" he asked.

"Paul!" my mom said.

Paul paused and strummed a few chords. "How 'bout this?" he said, and played Crosby Stills and Nash's "Our House," and we all sang along to the choruses. "Our house / Is a very very very fine house / With two cats in the yard / Life used to be so hard . . . " When the song was over I looked at my mother and saw that she'd been crying.

The next morning, I played quietly in my room while Paul slept on the couch in the living room. Chewbacca and Han Solo conversed in hushed whispers as they guided the Millenium Falcon onto my bed and Paul snored fitfully though the door. My mom made waffles which she piled up in the warmed oven as we politely waited for my uncle to wake on his own accord. Finally, the waffles could wait no longer and my sister and I were instructed to wake up our guest. We leapt onto his stomach and batted at his face with the couch cushions until he threw us off, grumbling.

We ate the waffles and my mother and sister went out and Paul and I were left alone. "Show me some of your records," he said.

I pulled out the two records I had been given for Christmas. I first showed him *Chicago 16* and he grimaced. He grabbed the sleeve from me and, flipping it over, began scanning the track listing. "I can't believe these guys are still around," he said, handing it back to me. "What's that one?" I showed him Men at Work's *Cargo* and he shrugged his shoulders. "They're all right, I guess," he said.

I said that I wanted to learn to play guitar. "Show me your hands," he said.

I held out my hands, palms out, fingers extended. He grabbed them and studied the fingertips; he pretended to measure the length of my fingers. "Yeah, maybe," he said. He reached over and grabbed a plastic mask of C-3PO that was lying on the couch and, pressing it to his face, he intoned in a near-perfect English accent: "I say, master Colin, I'm famished for lunch, aren't you?"

Paul left on Tuesday, as he had promised, and he gave my sister and I big hugs by his red Honda. I helped him load his guitar in the back of the car. He gave me a high five and I stood in the gravel driveway of the Ewing House and watched him drive away.

*　　*　　*

Later that summer, my mother began looking for a new house. The Ewing House was too small, she said. She took me along on her house hunts with her realtor. "You'll probably have to switch schools," she said as I stared out the passenger seat window of her Volkswagen Rabbit. "I'm not sure we'll find something near Central."

She eventually ended up buying a house on State Street, near the Capitol building. It had been my friend Josh's house before. I had once thrown a toy snare drum from the top of the staircase in the house and it had hit Josh in the lip. He had needed stitches after the incident. The house was painted an ugly mustard yellow and sat on the edge of a small hill. She was right—I did have to switch schools. And since my father had recently moved from the Rodney Street house, I had no reason to continue going to Central Elementary. I broke the news to Mark one night as we laid in our sleeping bags on his front lawn.

"That sucks," he said.

*   *   *

In my room at my mother's new house, the only way I could listen to music was on a small black clock radio. On Sunday mornings, I sat in bed and held the clock radio on my blanketed lap and listened to Casey Kasem's Top Forty countdown. I tried to wake up early enough to catch numbers thirty through forty, but usually I only woke in time for the last twenty-five. I followed the rise and fall of Wham and Duran Duran; I learned to distinguish the four different radio edits of Falco's "Rock Me Amadeus"—I even memorized the German rap breakdown in the song for the edification of my classmates. My pulse quickened at the drum roll before the first notes of the Number One song rolled across the wires.

At my friend Matt's house, we would record the Top Forty Countdown on his small radio/cassette player and then go back, dubbing our voices over Kasem's as we made our own announcements, observations, and long distance dedications.

*   *   *

A couple of months later, Paul came back into town. He was driving his little red Honda to Wyoming, to work with his brother Mark doing construction. At the kitchen table, Paul drank a beer and talked about the work. He said it was a big contract and Mark's company was making a lot of money; he would be getting paid well and he'd have a pile of cash by the time he made it back to Eugene for the school year.

"Did you bring your guitar?" I asked.

"Sure did," he said, "Don't think I'll be spending three months in the middle of buttfuck Wyoming without that guitar."

"Paul!" said my mom.

After dinner, Paul and I did the dishes. He told me stories about his life in Eugene. His roommate wrote songs and had taught him everything he knew on the guitar. "I don't know how he does it," Paul said, "He just sits down and these great songs come out."

I said I'd like to write a song.

"Maybe we should write one," he said.

"Really?" I said, placing a bowl carefully on the drying rack.

"Yeah, you write the lyrics and I'll put it to music," said Paul.

After the dishes were done, we sat in the living room and Paul played his guitar and we all sang the choruses to the songs we knew.

I woke up that night, sweating. My forehead was burning and my vision was swimming. I walked downstairs to my mom's room and pushed the door open. "Mom?" I asked, "I think I'm sick." She grabbed the thermometer from the bathroom and, shaking it, stuck it in my mouth, beneath my tongue. I tasted the cold metal of the tip of the thermometer and listened to Paul snoring in the living room. I had a fever, my mother told me. I was sent to bed and was told that I would not be going to school the next day. I was secretly thrilled, knowing that it meant a day alone with Paul.

The following morning, after my mother had gone to work and my sister to school, I lay on the couch and drank orange juice. Paul brought in his tape collection from the car and entertained me by playing DJ with my mother's tape deck. He played me Scritti Politti and New Order and Ultravox; he played a song called "88 Lines About 44 Women," and then said that he probably shouldn't have played it for me. I studied the tape cases as he played the cassettes, reading the names of the artists and songs quietly to myself in a litany. After he had exhausted his collection, Paul grabbed his guitar and we set about writing our song together. He plucked away at the twelve-string while I wrote lyrics in a note-pad. It was a song contrasting the lives of two types of musicians: one was a rocker, with wild hair and flippant attitude while the other was a classical composer. The verses were a "day in the life" approach to their vocations with the final line of the chorus tying their two disparate lives together: "And he liked his job." When I finished the lyric, I handed it to Paul. He looked it over and began making up a melody and chord progression behind the words. I was disappointed. Whereas I had imagined a hard, jagged feel to the arrangement, Paul had chosen a distinctly folkier approach. He sang the chorus as if it were a Bob Dylan song, even taking the liberty to repeat the last line of the chorus, the hook, a few times over in a singsongy voice. I feigned approval when he had finished.

That afternoon, Paul left the house to meet my mother for lunch downtown. He left me with his guitar and I sat on the couch, gingerly playing each string, listening for the changes depending on where I placed my fingers on the neck. By the time Paul had arrived back home, I had written a short, two note melody.

"Listen to this," I said as Paul walked in the door. I played the melody, my tongue inching out between my lips as I pressed my finger against the strings. When I had finished, I looked up at my uncle, expectantly.

"Oh, that's great," said Paul, facetiously, "That's real nice." He walked off into the kitchen.

Paul didn't last very long in Wyoming. He called my mother a month later, saying that he'd had enough; that he couldn't take any more. The pay was bad and he couldn't deal with the other guys on the job. He had packed up his Honda in the middle of the night and had driven back to Eugene in one shot.

During the first week of my fifth grade year, I had my mother drive me to Henry J's one evening. Browsing through the bins of records, I discovered Scritti Politti's *Cupid and Psyche '85*, recognizing the brown and red packaging from the cassette copy Paul had shown me. I insisted that my mother give me an advance on my allowance and bought it. In the car on the way home, I opened the sleeve of the record. A strong smell of clean plastic wafted up from the vinyl and I held the record close to my chest.

*   *   *

Whereas Central School had a tough, athletic student population, my classmates at Jefferson School were nerdy and creative. By fifth grade, I had shed the hardened exterior I'd developed after years of attending school with the kids who lived in the trailers up the Gulch and among the apartment buildings overlooking the bars on lower Rodney Street, opting instead to give in to my more effeminate, imaginative pursuits. I still played basketball, but became less troubled when my abilities began to fall behind those of my classmates. I began reading more, influenced mainly by Josh and his circle of friends, who had created a cult-like group fascination for fantasy books and comics. In a year, I had torn through the first eight books of Piers Anthony's *Xanth* series, each novel enjoying *Cupid and Psyche '85* as its ever-repeating soundtrack. Mark and I still saw a lot of each other, and he would tell me stories about all the kids I knew at Central while I tried to introduce him to whichever comic book or fantasy novel had my attention at the time.

One morning, Mark and I were sitting in his base-ment, watching television. I had stayed over the night before and we were eating Cheerios. There was a cop show on TV. Two criminals were fighting over their share of the loot. One of them pulled a gun.

"Kids are tough at Central," he said absently.

"Yeah?" I asked. I took another bite from my bowl of cereal, "I guess kids aren't very tough at Jefferson."

"That's what they say at Central," said Mark.

"That we're not tough?" I asked.

"Yeah," said Mark.

I paused for a moment, swirling my spoon through the leftover milk. "I guess they're right."

*   *   *

The next Christmas, I received a small and boxy package in the mail from Paul, and put it under the tree with the rest of the presents. Of all of them, I looked forward to opening it the most. All through breakfast, I tried to imagine what the present could be. When we finally sat down to open our gifts, Paul's was the first I picked. As I tore the wrapping away, I found a small black TDK cassette tape. I flipped it over and began reading the track listing, willing the tape to be filled with the likes of New Order and Ultravox, but was sorely disappointed: the tape chronicled the entire musical output of a local Eugene band called the Headhunters. The compilation was made up of a series of four to six song demos, recorded alternately in Coos Bay, Oregon, and Austin, Texas. Paul had written the names of the band members on the back of the insert and I recognized the name of the lead singer as being his roommate at U of O, the one who had such a knack for writing songs. I smiled halfheartedly and set the tape down by the ski gloves and wool socks that had started to accumulate at my feet.

Later that afternoon, while my sister went ice-skating and my mother was on a walk, I popped the Headhunters tape in my walkman. After fifteen minutes, I pulled the cassette from the player, placed it back in its case and shelved it away next to a dusty collection of 1940s radio dramas on tape.

It stayed there, untouched, for several months. At the time, my fascination with Scritti Politti had given way to a deep obsession with Depeche Mode, another discovery from the Top Forty Countdown, and I had painstakingly collected all of their records. I listened to them relentlessly, letting the auto-reverse function on my cassette player spin them into perpetuity until the length of tape at the beginning and end of the reel began to stretch and the opening synth lines warbled. I played them while I read my Xanth novels; I played them while I drew pictures of elves in my bedroom; I brought them with me when I traveled anywhere with my parents, immediately ejecting whatever Bonnie Raitt or Roches cassette had been in the tape deck in favor of *A Broken Frame* or *Some Great Reward*, prompting the following exchange with my mother:

> STEREO: (singing) *Hey you're such a pretty boy / Hey you're such a pretty boy / Hey you're such a pretty boy / You're so pretty.*
> MY MOTHER: Are these men gay?
> ME: Ummm, no. God, Mom!

At some point during my sixth grade year, *Black Celebration* (or some other part of the massive and ever-spreading Depeche Mode oeuvre) must have overstayed its welcome as I finally pulled my uncle's gift from its exile among the *Lone Ranger* and *Green Hornet* episodes. I sat down one afternoon and listened to the tape from start to finish.

It was simple stuff—two guitars, bass, and drums. Reminiscent of the Talking Heads, the Headhunters began as a strictly garage-bound band, recording their three-minute pop/rock songs on a four-track in Coos Bay. The tape followed their career as they broke free of their Oregon home and headed for Texas to record the middle five tracks of the tape. Somewhere in Austin, though, it was obvious that some sort of breakdown occurred, as the final four tracks of tape were accredited to the lead singer alone, stripped down versions of previous Headhunters songs, played on synthesizers and a drum machine.

What really grabbed me, though, were four songs that were stuck on to the end of the tape—an afterthought, really—by my uncle, who obviously had exhausted the entire body of work of the Headhunters within the first side-and-a-half of the cassette and needed some filler for the end. I decided that never had four so different songs been placed one after another, and yet, in the context of the tape, they seemed to match up perfectly. I sat up from my bed and clawed the cassette case into my palm from the bedside table and, tearing it open, I read the names and artists of these unearthed, nearly-forgotten songs. The first was "Pray For Rain," by Guadalcanal Diary, a band name I had to study for a moment before I was able to move my lips with the correct pronunciation; this was followed by Hüsker Dü's "Hardly Getting Over It," which lead into "Superman," by R.E.M. Paul had written "THE BEST BAND IN THE WORLD" under this last title. "I Will Dare," by the Replacements, was fourth, under which my uncle had written "THESE GUYS ARE GONNA BE HUGE." I listened most closely to this fourth song, to the chime of the guitars, the snap of the drums and the guttural growl of the singer's voice and I decided, yes, they are gonna be huge. I rewound the tape to the last Headhunters song and listened to the four sweeper tracks again. And again. And again. Until my head was ringing with the melodies.

That spring, I shelved my Depeche Mode fascination and began painstakingly tracking down each of the records the songs had been pulled from. R.E.M.'s record was the easiest—by the time I had discovered "Superman" at the end of the Headhunters' cassette, "The One I Love" had begun to seep into mainstream commercial radio. While none of the Helena radio stations acknowledged its existence, the video was in constant rotation on MTV and there was an actual, distinct R.E.M. section at Pegasus Music that boasted both *Document* and *Lifes Rich Pageant*.

Candy Apple Grey was Hüsker Dü's major label debut and I bought it the same day I bought *Lifes Rich Pageant*. Expecting more of the same acoustic guitar-based balladry as the track that first inspired me to buy the record,

I was completely thrown off-guard when "Crystal," the album's throat-tearing, amp-blowing opener, came bursting out of my Sony's speakers. I stopped the tape and pulled it out to make sure I had been given the correct cassette.

Gaudalcanal Diary was a little more difficult to track down, even though it, too, was a major label release. The boy working the counter at Pegasus glared at me as I pronounced the name while he wrote it down on an order slip.

"Say that again?" he said, scratching out whatever jumble of letters he had just written.

But they did have *Let It Be* in stock, and I bought it with Mark the day we spray painted "PUNK ROCK" on the plastic sled.

After that initial, exuberant introduction to the Replacements, I was allowed time to sink in to the record a little more on my own. Of all the records I had bought under the influence of my uncle's tape, it stuck with me the most. It became the soundtrack to the summer before I leapt headlong into middle school.

I learned to call this kind of music "College Rock." My mother had had a subscription to *Rolling Stone* since Lennon was shot—she had hung the cover, the one with the picture of the naked John embracing the supine, clothed Yoko, on the wall at our house—and in a corner of the back page, where the *Billboard* charts were listed, they printed the "College Charts." The source was usually some college radio station reporting the top spins of the week. *Pleased to Meet Me*, the Replacements' latest record, sat on top of the College Charts for several weeks before it was dethroned by Sinead O'Connor. I regularly began checking the *Rolling Stone* College Charts for new and interesting sounding bands. "Alternative music" was barely a catchphrase at this time. More common was "underground" or "Modern Rock," but I preferred the breezy erudition of "College Rock." I imagined short-haired, khaki'd college kids with big, circular tortoiseshell glasses, sitting around in dorm rooms, listening to this music while they studied from their massive textbooks.

My friend Colin reported to me one day that he had been riding his bike when a car pulled up beside him, blasting New Order.

"I think he was a college student," he said.

"Must've been," I said.

I envied Colin that moment. Carroll College, a small Catholic college on the west side of Helena, was the closest thing we had to a full-fledged university. There was no college radio station, however, and the school's curriculum favored pre-med and sports-related sciences. The college student I had invented in my mind, the one for whom *Rolling Stone*'s College Charts was expressly printed—the slacking, vinyl-collecting philosophy or liberal arts major—did not exist in great numbers in Helena. I began to think of them as rare aquatic birds, and Colin had managed a sighting.

I imagined that my uncle Paul was living the life of the mythical college student. From his stories, I pieced together a vivid world in which he spent his days, when not studying or in class, playing guitar with his friends and listening to records. Over the phone, he would regale me with stories of his college life: how he and his roommates would turn off all the lights in the dorm, put on an Ultravox record, light candles and lie on the floor, staring up at the ceiling; how he rushed out and bought *Lifes Rich Pageant* when it first hit the stores and ran home with it and played it five times in a row on his turntable; how he listened to the third side of Hüsker Dü's double LP, *Zen Arcade*, at a deafening volume when he had discovered a friend of his in bed with his girlfriend.

*   *   *

Paul called from Eugene pretty regularly. One Saturday morning, my mother answered the phone, and as soon as I realized it was him on the other end of the line, I ran into the living room and put one of my newly acquired tapes on the stereo at a volume that I figured he would be able to hear over the phone. *Let It Be* blasted from the stereo and my mom handed the phone over to me. I held the receiver in my hand for a moment, so he could hear what I was listening to, before I put the phone to my ear.

"Listening to the Replacements, huh?" he said.

"Oh," I said absently, as if trying to recall what I had put on the stereo, "Yeah, I guess I am."

"You like that record?" he said.

"Yeah, I like it pretty good," I said.

We talked about the Replacements for a bit. He said that the song "Sixteen Blue" perfectly encapsulated what it was like growing up for him.

"Just you wait," he said. "That's a hard year."

He told me that the bass player for the Replacements had been as old as I was when he first joined the band.

"Really?" I asked incredulously.

"Yeah," he said, "Paul Westerberg wrote 'Sixteen Blue' for him."

He told me how the Replacements had just played in Portland and had been so drunk that they could barely even get through the concert. They had insisted on going onstage wearing all of the clothes of the opening band on top of their own and they only played sloppy covers.

"When they're in bad form like that," he explained, "They call themselves the Placemats. Or the 'Mats, for short."

"Cool," I said.

He told me what he knew of the band, what he had learned from magazines. "They're from Minneapolis," he said, "Minneapolis, Minnesota."

What I knew of Minnesota I had gleaned from my parents' much beloved Prairie Home Companion broadcasts on NPR. NPR was ubiquitous in my mother's house particularly, where the stereo receiver dial seemed permanently affixed to Missoula's public radio station, and Garrison Keillor seemed to be its main spokesman. I envisioned a Minnesota very similar to Montana—small-town mentality, community-minded individuals, and plenty of snow in the winter. In my mind's eye, I imagined the Replacements, the four miscreants from the cover of *Let It Be*, practicing in a garage while the variegated characters from Lake Wobegon spouted time-honored Midwestern Lutheran wisdom in kitchens and cafes beyond. And somehow, the two seemed to meet.

The fact that the Replacements had to endure that sort of environment while trying to keep up a hard-case punk-rock image really appealed to my predicament. That they had to live through 40 below winters and frozen pipes, while surrounded by what I perceived as being a wholesome cultural backwater, brought the Replacements closer to me, closer to Helena, Montana. They seemed like the kind of band that could be practicing in my garage, my basement, and still be crunching out the same indelible music. The kind of band who would play at the local coffee shop or even at Hopper Daze.

*   *   *

The Helena Middle School sat at the north end of Rodney across the street from a triangular park where Rodney ran into Main Street. That summer before seventh grade, Mark and I rode our bikes past the school and stole glances into the darkened windows of the classrooms, the gymnasium and the auditorium. The football field was empty and we parked our bikes by the gate and hopped the fence. We acted like marathon runners, struggling the last few miles over the black rubber of the track that encircled the football field. We lay in the grass, staring up at the blue sky until the sprinklers came on and we sprinted for our bikes. We talked about how great it would be to be going to the same school again.

Mark had saved enough money that summer to buy a guitar he'd been watching at the pawn shop across the street from the Red Meadow. We rode our bikes there and Mark emptied his pockets of twenty-five one dollar bills on to the pawn shop counter and we rode back to his house with the guitar strapped over his shoulder.

I had some money, but not enough to buy a guitar. I had seen one at Bitterroot Music downtown—a glossy black hollow-body electric—but it was fifty dollars and well out of my price range. I had been drawn to it immediately upon seeing it; it was identical to the guitars I had seen slung over the shoulders of the geyser-haired members of the Jesus and Mary Chain.

We plugged Mark's guitar into his father's stereo with a curly instrument chord he had bought at Radio Shack and we took turns playing it. I showed him the song I had made up on my uncle's guitar and Mark said it was cool. We tried to get the guitar to distort by turning up the stereo but the speakers began to pop and shudder and Mark said we should turn it down.

"Let's start a real band," I said. "Not like the Babies, but a real band." Mark nodded in agreement.

That night I told my dad that I wanted to start a band and he said that I needed to learn to play an instrument. "Other than the clarinet," he added, referring to the instrument I had so half-heartedly taken up in school. I told him there was a guitar I was looking at buying but I was twenty dollars short.

"Better start mowing some lawns," he said. It was his answer to any money grumble I had.

Before too long, I had my guitar; my dad drove me to Bitterroot Music and I carried it out of the shop. Uncased, we brought it back home in the trunk of his car. Because it was a semi-acoustic, I couldn't play it through my dad's stereo and had to strum on it unamplified while I waited for Sears and Roebuck to deliver the $35 amplifier my uncle Steve ordered for me for my birthday. When it finally arrived, a little plastic thing, barely a foot tall, I retreated to my room at my dad's house and plugged in the guitar. At low volumes, the sound the amplifier produced was paltry, but when turned to the highest notch, the distortion was phenomenal. At the time, I had no working knowledge of how to create chords—what I knew was limited to the song I had invented on Paul's guitar. I did discover, however, that by strumming wildly while my plastic Sears and Roebuck amplifier was turned up to its highest volume, the sound it produced was spine-tinglingly close to the sound I had heard from my Replacements record, my Hüsker Dü record and my Jesus and Mary Chain record. I sat as in a trance, wildly hammering the strings of the guitar while the amplifier shook under its own volume until my dad screamed at me from downstairs.

"What?" I asked, sticking my head out of the door.

"What are you doing up there?" he asked.

"Just playing guitar," I said.

"Well, stop," he said, "We need to get you some lessons."

My mom knew of a guitar teacher I could go to for cheap. His name was Al Estrada and she had met him when he was teaching at a preschool in town. I vaguely remembered him; he used to sit and draw pictures of UFOs for me, gently instructing my attempts to do the same. At the time, he had long brown hair that he pulled back in a pony tail and I remembered that he often sang us to sleep during naptime while playing his guitar. He had lived on the Rodney Hill, in a small house above Mark's, during the early eighties. He was now living in a Victorian on Euclid and was looking for guitar students.

As I walked in the door of his top floor apartment, the heavy smell of incense hit my nostrils. He answered the door and ushered me in with a big smile. He had since cut his hair short and there were wrinkles around his eyes. He introduced me to his girlfriend, a tall dark haired woman, and explained that she was just leaving. She slipped into the bedroom of the small apartment and I sat down on the couch in the middle of the living room. The walls were covered with tapestries and Al's collection of guitars sat by the stereo.

"So," he said in introduction, "I guess we'll just start with some basics."

He taught me some rudimentary chord structures on my black hollow-body, and then he turned me loose with his pocket amplifier while he talked to his girlfriend in the doorway. The amp was the size and shape of a walkman. I plugged my guitar into the jack, put on the headphones, and was lost against a wall of distortion. I ran my introductory barr chord up and down the neck, noticing some marked similarities between my invented chord progression and over half the songs on *Psychocandy*. I was in awe of the possibilities. After about fifteen minutes, I felt a tap on my shoulder. I pulled off the headphones and saw Al nodding at me. "Ready for another lesson?" he said.

*   *   *

His name was Ryan and he was an eighth grader. He had straight blond hair and his bangs fell over his eyes in a diagonal line while the hair over his ears was shaved down to the skin. He was wearing a black trench coat with a long series of safety pins jutting out from the right sleeve. His lapel was covered with buttons advertising such bands as Suicidal Tendencies and 7 Seconds. He had sewn a piece of t-shirt cloth with the logo for the band DRI (a walk-signal stick figure in a slam-dancing pose) on the back of his coat, and his boots were Doc Martens that snaked up his calves with a myriad of eyeholes, tied tightly over the legs of his black jeans. His sticker-covered skateboard sat on end, propped against his knee. Mark had started talking to him on the street corner as we were walking home— Ryan knew Mark's sister—but I kept my distance, studying his get-up with a mixture of fear and admiration. I glanced down at my clothing: slightly tapered Levi's over clean white Nike shoes, an oversized Gotcha sweatshirt with small tribal-looking neon figures cavorting across the chest. I wandered closer. In a break in the conversation, I pointed to one of his band buttons and said: "I like the Suicidal Tendencies," even though I didn't, really.

"Yeah, me too," said Ryan. The video for "Institutionalized" had become a standby on *Post Modern MTV*, and I had watched it a few times, willing myself to relate to the hard-case, authority-hating nihilism of the song's protagonist. In the end, though, I couldn't bring myself to do it.

Mark looked at me and rolled his eyes. There was a rumor going around the middle school that Ryan had had anal sex with one of the seventh graders, Jennifer, and that she had had to wear a Maxi-Pad on her ass for several weeks after. It had boosted his image considerably. The Jennifer in question had recently taken me into her confidences by showing me, one day after school, a small bud of marijuana. She had held it cupped in her hands. "I'm gonna take this home," she said, conspiratorially, "And I'm gonna put it on the burner and suck all the smoke up." I had a difficult time imagining how that was going to work, but was overjoyed to have had such an intimate conversation with this infamous character.

Suddenly, a Ford truck swerved around the corner and came to a screeching halt on the street near us. The frame of the truck stood about four feet off the ground, towering over its massive wheels and the driver stuck his head out of the window. It was a high school kid; a Caterpillar baseball cap was perched on his head and he shouted at us: "What is this, some sort of faggot convention?" Peals of laughter could be heard from within the cab of the truck. Mark and I instinctively started to back away, pulling our backpacks tighter to our shoulders. My heart began beating madly.

Calmly, Ryan reached down and unzipped his black duffel bag, revealing a small baseball bat. My eyes widened, but before he could bring it out, the truck had already sped off, leaving clouds of dust and exhaust in its wake.

"What's that?" I asked, my heart rate slowing again.

He pulled the bat out and handed it to me. The words "HICK STICK" had been carved into the wood in jagged, lightning bolt lettering.

Later, as Mark and I continued walking, I said that I myself was a kind of skater.

"A kind of skater?" asked Mark.

"One that doesn't, you know, skate," I said. "I mean, I listen to the same kind of music as them."

Mark laughed. "That doesn't make you a skater," he said. "I mean, even if you did skate, I don't think anyone would call you a skater."

Later that night, I put on *Let It Be* and hopped around to "We're Comin' Out" as if I were at a punk show. I pogoed and slam-danced around my room, my arms swinging and my legs pumping, imagining my Nikes to be two steel-toed boots and my jeans to be covered in patches of punk bands. An imaginary flannel hung about my waste and I careened against the walls of my room.

The next day, I decided I would take my first step into Punk-ness and I pegged my jeans and stuffed the cuffs into the heels of my shoes. I walked downstairs, wondering if anyone would notice my transformation. My dad said nothing as he drove me to school. I stared down at my feet during the ride, imagining what sort of reaction I would get from my friends. I imagined a scenario in which Mark quietly registered the change in my dress and he began to treat me with a muted respect; in which, during lunch, the skater kids called me over to the far side of the middle school parking lot and we talked about music and how much we hated hicks and jocks; in which I became beloved among the malcontents.

My dad dropped me off in the park opposite the school. The front yard was swarming with kids parking bicycles, sitting on the grass, walking towards the double doors of the school. I paused as I watched my dad's Volvo disappear into the distance and then I stooped down and undid the peg in my pants. Seeing Mark wave to me, I hurried across the street the join him.

Later that week, in Mr. Fletcher's English class, we were assigned to give an oral presentation in front of the class. I chose to give a short biographical talk on Piers Anthony; Amy Ferguson, a recent convert to skater-dom, gave a talk on Posers. "Posers are people who pretend to be something they're not," she said matter-of-factly, shuffling a pile of note cards in her hand. "They wear the Doc Martens, the army pants, the Vision skatewear shirts, but really, they're just preppies in disguise."

At my third row desk, I blushed and looked out the window.

*   *   *

On my insistence, my mother caved in and bought a TV with cable. Our days of borrowing the neighbor's black and white television to catch such major network events as *V* and *Shogun* were at an end. Most importantly, we now had MTV. I braved the nattering of my mother to stay up well past my bedtime to watch *120 Minutes* at 11:00 on Sunday nights. For two hours, the programmers at MTV played videos exclusively by the bands that were dominating the college rock charts: the Cure, Depeche Mode, the Smiths and XTC. During the week, I would try to catch *Post Modern MTV*, the younger sibling of *120 Minutes* at its thirty minute length, but would often miss it because of its brevity. It wasn't long before it disappeared from the programming schedule, leaving the behemoth *120 Minutes* as the only remaining bastion of College Rock on MTV. I watched the show intently, hoping that each video would be from one of my new favorite bands. I found that even among this, the mainstream representation of the fringe, the Replacements were still on the margin. After seeing the video for "The Ledge," the lead single off of *Pleased to Meet Me*, I understood why: shot in stark, uncompromising black and white, the video was comprised of one shot: the various shoed feet of each of the Replacements, while the band members to whom they belonged sat on a couch. For a song that was obviously about teenage suicide, it was a pretty bizarre approach to video-making. In relation to everything else on MTV, it was a complete outcast. By 1988, video budgets were expanding exponentially, and even the more obscure acts, those who peddled their videographies to *120 Minutes*, shot big and pushed for flashy production in their videos. "Even though we've signed to a major label," the Replacements' video said, "we still don't give a shit."

On *Let It Be*, the song "Seen Yer Video" lays out the Replacements' approach to mainstream promotion in its one lyric: "Seen yer video / That phony rock and roll / We don't wanna know." I understood then: to make any other sort of video would be nothing short of hypocrisy.

Little did I know, it would be only a year before the Replacements would abandon much of their anti-authoritarianism in favor of a slicker, more industry-friendly image. *Pleased to Meet Me*, itself edging closer to the mainstream accessibility they had eschewed on earlier records, would be followed by the great act-cleaner-upper, *Don't Tell a Soul*. No sooner had this record hit the Sam Goodys of America than Paul Westerberg was being interviewed in *Spin*, talking about how they'd given up drinking, that they wanted to be a decent band, dammit. Whereas the intention was right—a thousand concert promoters across greater North America must have sighed in relief—the essence of the band seemed to dissolve with this concession. I had a poster on my wall—a color print-out my uncle had sent me—with a picture of a heavy-lidded Paul Westerberg, staring into the camera. Beside the picture was printed a succinct Westerbergian aphorism: "I've tried to be a punk, a rocker, a drunk. I've finally decided I'm an artist, godammit, an artist."

By the time I got to them, the Replacements' glory days were heavily on the wane. Even though 1990's *All Shook Down*, the band's swansong, received mostly glowing reviews at the time of its release, it's shelf-life hasn't measured up to the earlier records, especially *Let It Be*. Bob Stinson, the band's founding lead guitar player, had been out of the band for two years in 1988. The Replacements, while not receiving the attention due to them by the Cure and Depeche Mode-heavy video rotation on *120 Minutes*, were taking leaps and bounds in their national visibility; they were, however, only two years away from their dissolution.

*   *   *

Around midnight, about halfway into the program, the folks at *120 Minutes* would post the upcoming national tour dates for a handful of the bands that had been showcased on the program. I huddled close to the television, the volume turned low so as to not wake my mom, and watched as the list of dates and venues scrolled up the screen. Each band's itinerary would start on one of the coasts and then amble westward or eastward, traversing the great plains and the southern deltas to arrive at the opposite coast. There was one common element in each of the schedules: if a band were heading westward, the itinerary would take a superhuman leap right after a Minneapolis date, landing three days, sometimes a full week, later in Seattle. Heading eastward, the same gap was included: Seattle was followed by a vacuum of dates, on the other side of which the band would re-emerge in such far-flung places as Chicago or Denver or Iowa City. To the booking agents, managers, and MTV programmers, Montana might as well not exist. It seemed to serve only as a stretch of land, a platform on which the great Interstate 90 spreads, a pipeline from one lucrative market to another. I was in a constant state of bereavement. My grandmother got the *New York Times* and I would scan the Sunday section every week to see if there were any concert notices for my favorite bands. On the inside of my locker door at school I had a collection of clipped-out concert advertisements: Echo and the Bunnymen at Radio City Music Hall, Depeche Mode at Madison Square Garden, and an advertisement for a Replacements show at the Beacon

Theater, replete with a picture of the scraggly-haired foursome.

The bands that did come to town, the ones that were ambitious enough to launch a tour that included all of the lower 48 or had enough commercial radio visibility that would make a Montana appearance practical, were greeted with an enthusiasm that would be unmatched in any other entertainment-laden metropolis. Live performances by rock bands, regardless of their age or popularity, gave every like-minded pre-teen and teenager in the greater Helena valley area a chance to try out their musty, unused concert-going personas.

In 1987, just as the Replacements were touring the major cities of America in support of their latest record, the spandexed Canadian acapella troup, the Nylons, paid a visit to Helena, playing a concert at the Civic Center while promoting their latest output, *Happy Together.* The event was quite a sensation around the Middle School, and parents of enthusiastic pre-teens around the city dutifully shelled out the 20-odd dollars for tickets. The group had made a pretty solid showing on the *Billboard* charts with their 1984 hit "Na Na Hey Hey Kiss Him Goodbye" and were riding on the coattails of their second chart hit, an acapella rendition of the Turtles' "Happy Together." My mother had their latest record and I had heard their recent hit on the radio, but I was driven to go to the show more out of desperation to see live music. The show was packed; when the Nylons eventually took the stage, all unitards and mustaches, the entire population of the Helena Middle School rushed the stage, myself included, caught up in the excitement of a live performance. I stayed up front with my schoolmates, cheering during the song breaks, singing along to the songs I recognized. It wasn't until halfway through the concert, during a particularly steamy breakdown in which one of the members of the group walked downstage and, mugging for the audience, stuck his hand down his pants, grabbed his crotch, pulled his hand out and licked it, that I had a moment of epiphanic clarity. I glanced to my right and saw a classmate, a girl named Sarah, scream shrilly at this Nylon's sexually-charged gesture, and reach out for him, her eyes rolled back in her head in erotic desperation.

I had spoken with Sarah in the foyer of the Civic Center earlier that evening. She, like myself, was at the show largely on the insistence of her parents. She was only vaguely familiar with the Nylons through what little she had heard on the top forty radio stations in town. But here she was, screaming and weeping like this was 1964 and the four obviously flaming Nylons were nothing other than John, Paul, George, and Ringo. And yet there I was too, already a self-described music snob who had long thrown away his Boston and Robert Palmer tapes, cheering along with her. I was deeply ashamed. After the concert, I stood out in the empty parking lot as I waited for my father to pick me up and felt flushed with despair, thankful that there were none of the skater set at the concert—they, naturally, would not be caught dead at a Nylons concert.

*   *   *

Belmont was a ski hill about half an hour outside of Helena. It was relatively cheap and the snow was decent most of the year. My dad, in an effort to increase my number of group related sports activities, talked me into joining the Belmont Junior Ski Team. "It'll help you learn to work with people," he said. I was already bemoaning my seemingly needless participation on the Middle School's 7th grade basketball team—I spent the vast percentage of game time on the bench—so my dad figured this would be good alternative.

Practices were on Saturdays and a bus would pick up the team at the Colonial Inn at 8 a.m., delivering us to the bottom of the ski hill. It was a thirty-minute bus ride, during which I would have to listen to the hotshots on the team issue jocky challenges to each other and recklessly boast about their sexual escapades. I always brought my walkman along and stayed silent in the front of the bus, hoping to avoid any crossfire from the slung insults and challenges. I brought *Let It*

Be on these Saturdays, because it was ideal music to ski to, but there was an ulterior motive in that most of the record was loud enough to drown out my fellow bus-riders.

On the third Saturday of the season, the bus deposited us at the ski hill and we all marched up to the lodge where we prodded and shoved our over-stuffed ski bags into lockers and under benches. Then we were off to the top of the hill where the instructor was ready to give us our morning drills. We practiced kick turns and pole planting and then did some practice runs. I was sore, uncomfortable and quiet. Where my teammates absorbed our coach's instructions and improved with each run, I faltered as my movements came under increasing scrutiny. By the afternoon, when the rest of the team gathered together at the bottom of the course and trash-talked each other's runs, I stood apart on my own, afraid to join in and secretly thankful that no one was inviting me. The hours of practice inched along at glacial speed until the coach took me aside.

"How ya doin', Colin?" he asked. He was smiling, but his brow was creased with concern.

"I'm fine," I said.

"Maybe you want to hit free-ski a little early today?" he asked.

"Sure," I said.

"All right. See you next Saturday," he said, patting my back. Just as I was turning to ski off, he shouted, "Hey! Great job today! Keep working on those turns."

As I glanced to nod at him, I noticed the entire rest of the team, standing in a group, watching me ski away. One leaned over and whispered in another's ear. I shuddered with embarrassment. Back down at the chair-lift line, I put my headphones on and blasted *Let It Be*. "Wanna be something / Wanna be anything!" shouted Paul Westerberg and I spent the rest of the day tuning out the world.

* * *

When the spring hit and the snow had melted away and our seventh grade year was drawing to a close, Mark and I started spending time in the hills behind his house. Our camping and hiking acumen had grown considerably and we now packed for our overnighters in the meadow with a practical economy. We built a lean-to in a stand of trees overlooking the meadow and cobbled together a circle of rocks where we built massive bonfires; we whittled birch branches for roasting sticks and had hot dogs and s'mores on warm summer evenings. We bowed out of normal junior high weekend activities in favor of these short camping trips. I couldn't stand the basketball and football games that would take place on Friday evenings and Saturday afternoons. I was anxious and uncomfortable at the school dances, and I was rarely invited to classmates' parties. If Mark suffered under the same social inadequacies, he never let on. He stayed active in sports and even had a few brief trysts with girls. However, watching Monty Python movies at my mom's house or hanging out in his basement playing Dungeons and Dragons always seemed to trump whatever other plans Mark had going on during the weekend. I broached the subject one evening while we were sitting in our lean-to, poking at the dying fire. I had been quizzing him on the more popular kids in our class; he hung out with them every once and a while and knew of all their comings and goings.

"John just dumped April," he said, pushing a piece of wood closer to the fire, "She's pretty bummed out. They were at a party last weekend and she totally freaked out."

"Do you think I'm popular?" I asked.

He paused, thinking. "People know who you are," he conceded.

I was secretly thrilled.

"Do you think people like me?" I ventured.

"Yeah," he said. "I think so. I mean, they don't *not* like you."

"Cool," I said, and then: "You're kinda popular."

"I guess, maybe," he said.

"Do you ever think you might be less popular for hanging out with me?" I asked.

"I don't know," he said. "But I don't really care."

*   *   *

Eighth grade came on and with it, a host of new hurdles and heightened pressures. The obligation to go to school dances increased. The year before, I had been one of many kids who were too nervous or grossed-out to attend these dances, but now with the collective maturation of my entire class, I could no longer hide behind these excuses. As a consequence, my absence at dances was noted. Mark tried to talk me into going to the first dance of the school year.

"It's cool," he said as we walked down the hall after school. "All that happens is the music plays and all the guys stand at one end of the gym and all the girls sit in the bleachers. Every once and a while a slow song will come on and a few of the girls will come down and slow dance with some of the guys but mostly everybody just stands there looking at each other."

"Sounds stupid," I said. "What kind of music is it?"

Mark rolled his eyes. "They don't play punk rock, if that's what you're getting at. They play . . . I don't know . . . dance music."

"Bleagh," I muttered, sticking out my tongue, "I'd go if they played decent music."

"Yeah, right," said Mark.

After school, I wandered over to the gymnasium and stood by the door, watching the members of the Pep Club string brightly colored ribbon and streamers through the rafters. Two older looking kids were setting up the DJ station. One was standing out in the middle of the floor while the other tested the speakers, some bland Richard Marx hit blasting intermittently from the cones. Kids were starting to line up at the window of the school store to pick up their tickets and I wandered over and got in line, fishing my school ID out of my backpack. The events of the evening slowly unfolded to me while I waited my turn: I imagined my father dropping me off in front of the school that night; I imagined walking into the dark gymnasium, dressed in my finest Gotcha clothing and the stone-washed jeans that sat unused in my dresser-drawer because I was too shy to wear them; I imagined standing among the other boys, the popular boys, on one side of the gym, watching the swarm of girls in the bleachers, picking out the one I would ask to dance. Mark's statement of earlier that summer rang in my ears: "I mean, they don't *not* like you."

I turned and walked out, pocketing my school ID.

*   *   *

Through elementary school, I had always been tall for my age. Because of this, I was often recruited to play on the basketball team. My dad had enjoyed a bit of fame in his junior high and high school days as a basketball player and he enthusiastically supported me when I went out for try-outs. Even though my raw ability on the court left a little to be desired—I was slow and clumsy and could not take my eyes off the ball when I was dribbling—I was always a shoe-in because of my height. By eighth grade, however, most of the kids who regularly went out for the basketball team had caught up or surpassed me in height. I was relegated to positions other than center in the try-outs—positions that required more skilled strategies than my "stand-under-the-basket-and-get-the-rebound" approach to being a center.

Mark and I went to try-outs on the same day. We were immediately separated in the first round when Mark was selected to vie for a position on the first-string team; I was sent to the other side of the gym. Over here, there were two types of contenders: kids like myself who were there more out of parental obligation or as a matter of habit than for any real love of the game; and aspiring jocks who had been rejected in the first round for the main team. This convergence was a terrible thing: the former group were beginning to realize they were not cut out for the sporting life, and the latter were overcome with bitterness and resentment, and were likely to take it out on their inferior teammates.

During our first practice, I was on the receiving end of this resentment. We had just split the team into skins and shirts for a scrimmage—as luck would have it, I had been selected for the skins team and reluctantly peeled my shirt from my skinny, pale chest. I had been worried about this, as I was very sensitive about the state of my physique at the time. Also, I had a common abnormality in my ribcage—a protruding zyphoid, a pea-sized piece of bone jutting from my sternum. I was placed as a forward and my opposing team member was a red-haired kid named Nick. Because all of his friends had made the first-string team, Nick was a red-haired, fat-headed ball of holier-than-thou attitude and had spent the entire practice thus far showing off his dribbling skill and taking needless three-point shots during earlier scrimmages.

As soon as play started and I was guarding him, Nick started making fun of my protruding zyphoid. "What's that?" he asked, "Your third nipple?"

I desperately tried to come up with an adequate comeback, and scanned his body for some sort of physical deficiency I could poke fun at, but either he had none, or I was too on-the-spot to find one. I froze and tried to ignore him. He grinned at me. There were beads of sweat balling up on his upper lip and I thought to myself, "What's that? Did you spit on yourself?" but refrained from saying it aloud, all too aware of how lame a retort it would be.

After practice, I caught up with Mark, whose team had been practicing on the other side of the gym.

"How'd you like it?" he asked as we stuffed our gym clothes into our lockers.

"I didn't," I said.

That night in my room, I laid on my belly and stared at the whirring capstans inside my Sony Sports boombox, the now well worn cassette of *Let It Be* within, while "Unsatisfied" blared through the speakers. I fought back the tears.

*   *   *

All through eighth grade, my uncle continued to send me tapes of the music he was discovering while living in Eugene. He sent me Robyn Hitchcock's *Globe of Frogs* backed with Camper Van Beethoven's *Our Beloved Revolutionary Sweetheart* on a single TDK SA-90 and I ate the stuff up voraciously. Paul rarely sent mixes; mostly it was two albums linked on a single cassette, with a few songs thrown on the end to make up for dead tape. Sometimes the combination of the two bands would clash stylistically (Cowboy Junkies' *Trinity Session* backed with Donner Party's eponymous second record) but within the context of the TDK, it made perfect sense. Mostly Paul would send me the tapes un-prompted; sometimes he would ask me for requests; one time, he sent a tape wholly on accident—expecting to receive a collection of early Robyn Hitchcock songs, I tore open a package from Paul and discovered an unlabeled cassette. Assuming it to be empty, I threw the tape on my boombox and was surprised to find the tape was filled. The music was obviously dated—the vocal delivery, the drums and guitars all sounded like they were lifted from the mid-seventies—a music that was completely unlike my collection at the time. And yet the fact that it had a place in my uncle's record collection kept me with it. The third song, a gorgeous acoustic number, stuck out to me. It began with the line "Won't you let me walk you home from school / Won't you let me meet you at the pool . . . "

I talked to my uncle later that week. "Oh," he said when I brought up the unlabeled cassette, "I didn't mean to send you that, sorry. You can send it back if you want."

"I kind of like it," I said, "Who is it?"

"You like it?" he said, "That's Big Star. The Replace-ments sing about them, you know. That song 'Alex

Chilton' is about them." He sang the bridge to me over the phone: "I never travel far / Without a little Big Star."

In the absence of song titles, I had made up my own and written them on the cassette's insert. On the other end of the line, he read the names of the songs of the record jacket and I read him what I had invented.

"September Gurls," he said, "That's 'gurls' with a 'u.'"

"I have 'December Boys Got It Bad.'" I responded. He laughed through the receiver.

Fittingly, the song that I had loved so much on first listen was called "Thirteen": "Maybe Friday I can / Get tickets for the dance . . . " Though I had yet to attend a dance, much less ask a girl to one, the line still gave me the melancholy shivers. I began to wonder if I would ever ask a girl to a dance.

*   *   *

At home, I was listening to music like it was medicine. As soon as I got home from school, I would head upstairs to my room and press play on my Sony Sports cassette player. The room would fill with music and I would lie on my bed, staring at the constellations of glow-in-the-dark green spots that covered my ceiling in an inexact replica of the cosmos. My mother and I had spent an afternoon covering my ceiling with the spots while listening to *The Queen is Dead* on repeat on my stereo. My mother said all the songs sounded the same. And again, she wondered if they were gay.

"No, mother," I said—though this time, I was less convinced myself.

I listened to *Let It Be* endlessly. The record seemed to encapsulate perfectly all of the feelings that were churning inside me. The leap from seventh to eighth grade had felt like a quantum shift and my head was reeling from the changes. My eccentricities were becoming more and more pronounced against the status quo of my schoolmates. I was fitting in less and less. I'd been told by older classmates that middle school girls were easy, but I could barely bring myself to speak with them, let alone try to get in their pants.

Your age is the hardest age
Everything drags and drags
Think it's funny? You ain't laughin' are you
Sixteen blue
Sixteen blue

Paul Westerberg's weary voice sounded from my boombox and I trembled to think that here I was, thirteen, and the "hardest age" was still three years in the making. I felt like yelling at the stereo, "Well, thirteen ain't so easy either!"

My guitar lessons were one saving grace. I arrived at the door of Al Estrada's apartment every Monday night to be taught new chord structures and scales on my black hollow-body guitar. One day I showed up and Al told me that he'd decided I was ready to move on.

"Move on?" I asked.

"You know, take the next step," he responded. "I have a brother who's an amazing guitar player. I mean, really amazing. He goes on tour with rock bands all the time. He gets hired by other guitar players to teach them songs. I mean, he's really good."

"Okay," I said, though I honestly didn't feel like I'd taken any steps at all. I was still struggling with some of the more rudimentary guitar techniques.

Al's brother lived in the Stuart Homes and when my dad dropped me off in his cul-de-sac the next week, I half expected to see lovely Lynette come walking out from one of the carsick-green houses. I marched up to the door of the apartment and knocked. Al's brother answered. He was tall and gangly and he had long, stringy black hair that hung over his shoulders. He was wearing a tank top and a thin gold chain around his neck and he invited me in.

"Hi, dude," he said.

"Hi," I said. I hadn't ever been called 'dude' before.

On the phone earlier that week, he had told me that the way he preferred to teach guitar was by having his students bring in music they'd like to be taught. He said they absorbed the lessons better. He brought out his guitar—a bright purple thing with jagged edges—and said, "So, what do you got for me?"

Reaching into my backpack, I pulled out three tapes: *Louder Than Bombs*, *Never Mind the Bollocks*, and *Let It Be*. He shuffled through them wordlessly as I took my guitar out of its case.

"I never heard of any of this stuff," he said. "But whatever."

We started with the Replacements. I wanted to learn "Sixteen Blue." He listened quietly, tugging at strands of his hair and toying with his gold chain. He played a few chords on his guitar and said, "I think I got it" and he showed me the chords. We played the chords together for a moment. I could hear the melody beginning to surface from beneath what I was playing and I was ecstatic. I nodded in appreciation to Al's brother and he smiled, though it was obvious that he found the simplicity of the song's arrangement tedious. He showed me the chords to the chorus and then said, "And then it sounds like the dude solos . . . " he paused for a moment, listening to Bob Stinson's heavenly, understated solo, "But that's kind of a pansy solo. Try this on for size—

here, play along." He then began playing frantic, lightning-fast arpeggios up and down the neck while I played the two chords of the verse.

After that, we moved on to the Smiths. I wanted to learn "Unloveable," the mid-tempo number at the end of side two. Al's brother listened to it quietly.

> *But I know that you would like me*
> *If only you could meet me*
> *If only you could see me*

Morrissey moaned plaintively and Al's brother listened. He mashed his fingers on to the neck of his purple guitar in a myriad of arrangements, trying to fit his fingers around Johnny Marr's delicate guitar work.

> *I know I'm unloveable*
> *You don't have to tell me*
> *Message received loud and clear*

"Umm," said Al's brother after the song had faded to a close. "Might have to listen to that one again." For the rest of the lesson, Al's brother listened to "Unloveable" over and over again, each time trying to figure out the chord structuring. Finally, when the hour drew to a close, he conceded victory to Johnny Marr. "Bring me something else next week," he said.

This followed week after week. Within a month, I had Camper Van Beethoven's "She Divines Water," Hüsker Dü's "Flip Your Wig," and the lead track from *Let It Be*, "I Will Dare," under my belt. At home, I practiced incessantly, crunching the chord changes to the songs over and over until they were ingrained in my fingertips. "Unloveable," however, continually stumped Al's brother's prowess. We tried it a few times more over the month, but each time he was frustrated. He finally gave up completely and I was never allowed to mention the song again in practice.

One spring Monday, into the fifth week of my lessons with Al's brother, I dutifully showed up at the Stuart Homes, a fresh stack of tapes in my backpack, their chords and melodies waiting to be revealed. I knocked on the door and was surprised when a woman answered. She was my height and wore a shock of platinum blond hair. She was wearing the same green paisley pajama bottoms that Al's brother often wore during our lessons.

"Hi," she said.

"Hi," I said. "I'm here for my lesson."

"Oh," she said, looking surprised. "Um . . . he's gone."

"Gone?" I asked.

"Yeah, he left town."

"Oh," I said. She stared at me, silently, and fidgeted in the doorway. It became obvious that the information she had already given me during the exchange was all I was going to get.

I stammered: "I . . . I have a check for last week's lesson."

"Okay, I'll make sure he gets it," she said, extending her hand. I reached into my pocket and handed her the check, signed by my father.

I thanked her and she closed the door. Guitar in hand, I slouched off towards Montana Avenue to walk home.

*   *   *

While I was busy consuming *Let It Be* from end to end, there was still one song that I couldn't quite get: "Black Diamond." From what I understood of the precepts of college rock—and its forebears, punk and new wave— this music was supposed to stand in opposition to the proto-metal movement of the late seventies, early eighties. Bands like Van Halen, Led Zeppelin, and Judas Priest, with their sonic walls of reverbed-out drums, fiery guitar solos and shrill, soulless vocals, were the enemy. "Black Diamond" sounded like a paean to this movement and I was disappointed to find out that it was, in fact, a cover of a Kiss song.

I wasn't that familiar with the Kiss oeuvre—what I knew of them I learned from their short-lived television show, an episode of which I watched while at a family reunion in the late seventies. I had never liked metal as a kid, and with my newfound music snobbery, I loathed it even more. I couldn't understand why a band like the Replacements, capable of releasing such glorious material as the rest of the songs on *Let It Be*, would put a Kiss cover on their record. It was like they had created something truly beautiful and couldn't stop themselves from smudging it up a bit.

Ray was a kid in my Social Studies class and he was a self-described metalhead. He didn't hang out with the other denim-clad stoners who spent their lunch periods across the street in the triangle park, smoking cigarettes and blaring Megadeth from boomboxes, but he did have longish hair and a notebook covered with penciled re-creations of the Metallica logo. What's more, he was amiable—another quality that distinguished him from the undiluted variety of metalhead—and we would talk after class about bands.

He knew "Black Diamond," but not the Replacements version of it. He said I should watch MTV for Metallica; they had a new video out for a song called "One" that was about a soldier in the first world war who had had his arms and legs blown off by a bomb. The premise sounded enticing.

Against my better judgment (my anti-metal biases firmly in place), I did watch MTV that week for the

"One" video and managed to catch it. It was dark and seedy and the band members' faces were snarling and shadowed. I came back to the Social Studies class reporting to Ray that I was intrigued.

"Why don't you come over to my house after school?" he asked. "I'll play you some of my metal records."

I agreed and we met at the bike racks at 3:30. While we walked, we talked about the bands we listened to: I talked up Hüsker Dü, citing Bob Mould's stereo-melting guitar sound as a reason Ray might be interested; he talked about the relative merits of Judas Priest and Whitesnake. He was wearing a Poison t-shirt and I kept marveling over how much the members, all male, looked like tarted-up ladies. When we arrived at his house, he immediately ducked into his closet and changed his shirt. His mom called from the bottom of the stairs.

"Ray?" she called, "Are you home?"

"Yes, Mom!" he replied, walking out of the closet wearing a blue and white checkered button-up in place of his Poison shirt. He walked out onto the landing and waved at his mother. When he came back in, he looked relieved.

"She didn't see me," he said.

"What?" I asked. "The t-shirt?"

"Yeah," he said. "My mom and step-dad are serious Christians. I'm not allowed to wear that shirt."

He explained that the same rule that made it taboo to wear a Poison t-shirt also forbade him to listen to music that was not sanctioned by Christian groups. A few months ago he had been the victim of a shakedown in which his mother and their pastor went into his room while he was at school and threw away all of his Metallica and Judas Priest tapes. The scourge had left only his modest collection of Petra tapes—a band that professed to play metal, but with strong Christian sensibilities.

We sat on his bed and he played me a Petra record. The music was shiny and flaccid—the lyrics were, at best, sentimental and fluffy. It was metal to all intents and purposes—present were the minor key ballads and gated drums—but was obviously a crass imitation. Ray looked a little embarrassed that he had misled me.

I played him *Candy Apple Grey* and fast forwarded to "Black Diamond" on *Let It Be*. He was dismayed. "That's not what Kiss sounds like at all," he said. "Those guys kind of suck."

*   *   *

One morning in the spring, as I paged through the latest issue of *Rolling Stone* in homeroom, the principal came on with his daily announcement. Among the listings for pep rallies, dances and sports events, the voice announced that there would be auditions held on Friday for the school's spring musical production, which was to be *Guys and Dolls*.

"Are you trying out?" someone asked me, an acquaintance from the class.

"I doubt it," I said, returning to my magazine.

As the week wore on, I kept thinking of the audition. I asked my mom about the show.

"I saw the movie when I was a kid," she said. "It's about gamblers in Chicago, I think."

I had had a short fling with the theatre when I was younger; in sixth grade, sensing that my interest in athletics was on the wane, my mother signed me up for the local community theatre's after-school program. I had been excited about it at first—considering ways in which to mount a revival of my own theatrical effort, *The Bloody Knight*, on a larger stage—but was quickly disappointed. We had worked for weeks on a short, impressionistic acting exercise about the color yellow in which I spent the entire time on the floor of the stage in a fetal position, waiting for the moment to intone my one line: "I am a bit of pus."

On Friday after school, as I was pulling my backpack from my locker, I ran into my friend Spencer, a seventh grader, who was on his way to the auditions. "You're trying out?" I asked.

"Yeah," he said. "You should come too. It'll be fun."

I tagged along and joined the crowd of kids on the stage of the auditorium, staring out into the blackness of the theater while a disembodied voice asked us each, one after another, to say "Why, I oughta knock your socks off" in our best Chicago gangster accent. I was nervous and unsettled and my Chicago melded into Irish for a few vowels and I was given the part of Big Jule, a part with very few lines, but one that required an actor that towered above the rest of the cast.

Most of my eighth-grade classmates were too cool to try out for the show, so the vast majority of the parts were given to bright-eyed, over zealous seventh graders. Spencer was given the lead, Nathan Detroit, and he was the only person I knew in the entire cast. I spent the rehearsals, when not on stage, sitting in the wings with my walkman on. The soft plink of the opening chords of "Androgynous" spilled from my headphones as Adelaide and Nathan argued over his gambling habit.

> *Here comes dick, he's wearing a skirt*
> *Here comes jane, y'know she's sporting a chain*
> *Same hair, revolution*
> *Same build, evolution*
> *Tomorrow who's gonna fuss*

While on stage, I was shy and let other kids upstage me. I sang uncomfortably in a low register. One of the other eighth-graders in the production was a girl named Phoebe; she was a chorus girl and an understudy for Adelaide. I had a heart-wrenching crush on her, but was totally unable to communicate it.

I spoke with Spencer one evening after rehearsal. As a seventh grader, he was relatively popular and seemed to have no difficulty talking to girls. I asked him his advice.

"I don't know," he said. "Just talk to her." Even he seemed put off by my complete lack of social grace.

On opening night, there was a party at the director's house. My dad dropped me off at the door and I wandered in, still wiping stage makeup from my face. Phoebe was standing by the punch bowl, talking with some seventh-graders. I walked over, intending to say hello, but only managed to excuse myself while I grabbed a glass of non-alcoholic punch near her left elbow.

Joe, a minister's son, was sitting at the top of the stairs in the living room, playing an acoustic guitar to a group of girls who sat crowded below him. I wandered over to where they were sitting and listened in; he was playing "Every Rose Has Its Thorn," by Poison, and I cringed. Phoebe wandered over to the stairs and joined in with the crowd that had gathered.

After a few more songs, Joe put the guitar down and wandered off to refill his glass of punch. The group of girls that had gathered at his feet began to disseminate. On impulse, I picked up the guitar and began plucking at it. A few of the audience members lagged, including Phoebe, who sat down on the bottom stair and looked up at me.

Mustering all my bravery, I shut my eyes began playing a choice selection of songs I had been taught by Al's brother. I played "Sixteen Blue" and "God Save the Queen"; I played "Good Feeling" by the Violent Femmes, even humming the closing violin line. When I opened my eyes again, only a few of the girls were remaining, and most were talking amongst themselves. Phoebe had gone.

"Do you know 'Patience'?" one asked.

Before I had time to answer, Joe was back from the punch bowl and I dutifully handed him the guitar back. A few of the girls wandered back to the stairs and I walked off to the kitchen, where the rest of the gamblers were making fart noises with their armpits.

*　　*　　*

Paul called one Sunday evening in April. My mother answered; I was sitting on the couch, reading, when I recognized that it must be him. I dashed into the living room to put my Robyn Hitchcock tape on the stereo. After a few moments, she handed the receiver to me.

"Hey Paul," I said.

"Hi," he replied. He paused, then: "Listening to *Globe of Frogs?*"

"Yeah," I said. "I guess I am."

"What do you think about coming down here to Oregon this summer?" he asked. "Y'know, have a little coming-of-age time with your uncle."

"Really?" I asked.

"Yeah, I'll come pick you up; we'll drive down to Eugene. I think I can get you some work on the vineyard down here. Make a little extra cash for the summer."

"Sounds great," I said. He was living outside of Eugene on a vineyard that some friends of his owned. They were building a house on the property and Paul was living there while it was being built.

"We'll get you a pack of tapes and set you up with my record collection. That ought to give you something to do," he said, laughing.

With this on the horizon, spring passed achingly slowly. Finally, in June, I was sitting on the window seat in the living room of my mother's house when Paul's silver Toyota Tercel pulled up. I watched him pull the case of a guitar from the hatchback and walk towards the house. When I opened the door to him he said, "Ready to become a man?"

Paul stayed a few days in town. He even drove out to the valley and visited with my dad. He had graduated from the U of O a few years earlier and was keen to show off his new-found independence and maturity to his Montana relatives. On the day before we left for Oregon, we were sitting around chatting after breakfast when he suggested that we take his Tercel for a spin around town.

I hopped into the passenger seat; the back seat had been put down to make room for the two shelf speakers my uncle had installed in place of car speakers. "Listen to this," he said as he started the car. He popped a tape into the deck and out came Jane's Addiction's *Nothing's Shocking*. It blared from the shelf speakers, rattling the seatbelt casings and the windows and I saw my mother peek through the blinds of the living room window. "It's my metal record," shouted my uncle over the din of guitars and drums. "I find one every once and while. It's always good to have a metal record in rotation."

I nodded and smiled. I rolled down the window as we pulled away from the curb and started driving down

State Street. Near the intersection of State and Rodney we passed a kid from my Life Science class, riding his bike. As we drove by, he stopped and watched us, a cloud of music surrounding the small Toyota. I waved at him and hung my elbow out the window, feeling the sun beat against my arm.

We left for Oregon the following day. The air was clear and bright and I was enthralled to be leaving Montana. As passenger, it was my job to dig through my uncle's overstuffed tape case for music. The spines of the cassette cases were all illustrated by my uncle in colored markers. The names of the bands and their album titles sprawled out in blocky, colored-in lettering. Many of the bands I recognized: The Replacements were a big fixture, as was Robyn Hitchcock, Camper Van Beethoven and Hüsker Dü; but there were several I didn't recognize at all. I rarely made the decision as to what music we would listen to. Paul would command that I open the tape case and he would reach in and pick out a cassette. We weren't a half an hour on I-90, heading west, when my uncle had me reach into the side pocket of the tape case and pull out a small zip-lock baggie filled with pot. I was speechless, having only been in such close proximity to the drug when Amy showed me the small bud in her cupped hands. I tried to cover my anxiety by appearing unphased, but Paul took my silence as a judgment. "What?" he asked. "You got something against a little weed? Don't tell me you've never smoked it."

I lied. "I have," I said. "Just once. No big deal."

"Well, you're not smoking it on this trip," he said, grabbing the baggie from my hand. "If it ever got back to your mom, she'd kill me."

We arrived in Spokane that night and met with Paul's high school friend Dan. They drank vodka in Dan's high rise apartment while I looked through magazines on Dan's couch. They talked about the Clash; they showed me a photo of the two of them the summer after their graduation. They were both standing shirtless in front of a car that had "The Clash" spray painted on driver-side door. They were both holding beers.

"You still listening to that stuff?" Dan asked Paul.

"Yeah, you?" Paul replied.

"Nah," he said. "I don't have time any more."

Paul dug through Dan's record collection, commenting on its obvious lack of use. "Shit," he said, "You should give these away, give them to someone who's going to use them."

Dan shrugged in the kitchen and poured more vodka into his glass.

That night, they left me in Dan's apartment with a stack of old seventies punk records to cycle through while they went to the dog track. I listened to the Gang of Four, the Sex Pistols and the Buzzcocks on Dan's stereo and flipped through the collection of Playboy magazines he kept under the coffee table. I was asleep when they got back to the apartment; I woke up to Paul and Dan laughing and swearing. They knocked over a lamp in the dark and I heard it crack against the side of a table.

We left the following morning and drove to Seattle. At my uncle's insistence we listened to a collection of Bob Dylan bootlegs that spanned two 90 minute cassettes. I objected briefly, saying how I always thought Dylan was my parents' music and was boring.

"Dylan's very punk rock," Paul explained. "Without Dylan there would be no punk. There would be no Replacements." We listened to *Let It Be* after that, rocking our heads in unison to the songs, shouting along to the verses of "Answering Machine" as the flats of eastern Washington hissed by the window of the silver Tercel.

My courage is at its peak, you know what I mean
How do you say okay to an answering machine
How do you say goodnight to an answering machine

We drove through downtown Seattle, listening to the college radio station. They were playing a song by a band called Skinyard. "This station is funny," Paul explained. "They'll play two Skinyard songs followed by an Al Green song."

We stopped at a record store and wandered through the aisles. The walls were covered with rock posters and t-shirts, the sun slanting through the concert flyers that curtained the windows. Paul pointed out records that he had sent me. I pulled them out of their bins and studied them, registering every detail from the artwork to the band photographs, down to the lettering of the song titles. Paul talked to the clerk; after a few minutes of browsing, I joined them. The clerk, who was lanky and wore a ratty black Green River t-shirt, was talking about the indie label Sub Pop. "It's very hot right now," he said.

We left the record store and Paul stopped at a payphone to call a friend of his in town. His name was John and he had played in a band with Paul in Eugene. When we arrived at his apartment, he was in the process of reorganizing the P-S section of his record collection, which alone took up a good four feet of wall space. An entire wall of his living room was devoted to his mammoth record collection, housed in homemade pine shelving. I gaped as I walked in. John looked up from the pile of records covering his floor and invited us in.

"This is my nephew," Paul said, and I shook John's hand.

Paul explained that John's brother had been the guitar player in the Headhunters. "Very cool!" I said, which made John laugh.

We sat in his living room and talked while he continued to sort through the pile of records at his feet. John was a music critic for a local newspaper and was always being sent records for review. He put on a record by Yo La Tengo that he'd just received. We all listened quietly as he played it. Paul said it sounded like the Velvet Underground. John nodded in agreement. I stayed quiet and listened to them talk over the pulse of the music.

That night we stayed at another college friend of Paul's and left the following morning for Eugene. We had lunch at a pizza place by the college. While we ate, Paul craned his neck to look into the booth behind me, recognizing some guys he had known in the dorms. They were in a band called the Corp, Paul explained, and they played a sort of Red Hot Chili Peppers-styled funk. We walked over to them once we had finished and Paul said hello, shaking their hands and slapping them on the back. There were four of them. "How's the band?" Paul asked.

"Great," one of the men said. "We're playing tonight."

"Cool," said Paul. "We're in town for the evening. Maybe we'll stop by."

Outside on the street, I squinted up at Paul through the late afternoon shine of the sun. "I'm fourteen, Paul. How am I going to get into a bar?" I asked.

"We'll figure it out," he said. "I know the owner of the place they're playing."

We walked down 13th Avenue to a record store in a small, single-level house. Paul knew the owners and he introduced me to them. "This is my nephew," he said. I smiled and shook their hands; the constant stream of introductions I was receiving was beginning to feel routine.

That night, I waited outside the bar while Paul went inside. I watched through the plate glass as he approached the bartender. The band was warming up and I could hear people talking loudly over the din. Finally, after about fifteen minutes of waiting, Paul appeared at the door. "Come on in," he said.

I stiffened my back and pulled my shirt straight. "What did you do?" I asked.

Paul winked and said, "Never underestimate the power of pot."

The band had now begun its set and Paul and I walked over and sat in a booth. Soon, a steady stream of people began walking in the door, and Paul waved some of them over to where we were sitting. More introductions took place—a woman who sat across from me let me sip on her beer. The music was fast and danceable and Paul was soon up on his feet and dancing with some of his friends. I sat in the booth and watched until our table had been emptied of everyone except for me. I sipped at a beer that had been left behind and watched the crowd of dancers. Finally, Paul came over and squatted down next to me, catching his breath.

"That girl over there," he said, pointing to one of the dancers. She had long brown hair pulled back in a braid and wore glasses. "She wants to dance with you."

"Really?" I asked in disbelief. I felt a surge of nervousness that was quickly engulfed by a similar surge of embarrassment over the realization that I was probably a charity case, sitting at the booth by myself, sipping other people's beers. "Nah," I said. "I think I'll just hang out here."

"Come on," said Paul.

I grimaced.

"Do what you want," he said, dismayed, and he walked back to the dance floor.

Steeling myself, I got up on my feet and wandered over to where everyone was dancing. Having only ever danced alone in my bedroom to Smiths records, I watched the rest of the dancers' movements, searching for an example to follow. I began swaying my arms and shuffling my feet on the hard wood floor. I heard someone whistle; the music picked up and I could feel the crowd close in around me. I closed my eyes and continued dancing.

*   *   *

The house Paul was living in was on a small plot of land outside Monroe, Oregon. One square acre of grapevines constituted the vineyard. The house was an unfinished shell. Only the kitchen, the upstairs living room, and the bedroom had been insulated and sheetrocked. I slept on the floor of the living room, next to the stereo. In the morning, Paul left for work and I was left alone with his record collection.

I had bought a 12-pack of blank tapes at a Fred Meyer in Eugene and now I had them separated out on the floor of the living room as I started picking out records from Paul's collection. I pulled records from the shelf and stacked them in twos, matching up records by their compatibility on opposing sides of a tape. The Sex Pistols met the Sugarcubes in an unholy matrimony; the Gang of Four found themselves along side the Long Ryders. I spent the good part of an afternoon piecing together the entire recorded history of Hüsker Dü, pausing only to have lunch, and I inked the names of the bands on the spine with colored markers.

I found a wealth of Replacements in Paul's collection. Here were all the records I had amassed in my own collection but in glorious large format vinyl and CDs with insert booklets to read. But here still were records I hadn't heard: an EP called *Boink!* and the single for *Let It Be*'s lead track, "I Will Dare." I pored over the text on the inner sleeve of *Let It Be*, reading the production credits like they were poetry, gazing at the scrappy photographs, puzzling out the graffiti on the van wall in the background photo until Paul came home from work.

He laughed when he saw me, cross-legged on the floor, surrounded by a pile of vinyl records and blank cassettes. "You've spent all day doing this, haven't you?" he asked.

*   *   *

I still have all the tapes I recorded from my uncle that summer. Some are too old to play any more, most I have replaced with CD copies that have in turn been encoded into MP3 format on my computer's hard drive. *Let It Be* is now a mere click away. All of my old tapes now lie in a cardboard box in my closet, and serve only as a reminder of my younger days. From time to time, I'll pull out a mix tape I made in junior high and I'll play it—my girlfriend kids me that the mixes are essentially the same sort of compilations I would make today. That music feels like a hinge to me, the touchstone for all my musical meanderings, and a standard by which all subsequent discoveries must be measured. I still get a lot of play-time out of *Let It Be*; though quite a bit less than when I was in Middle School. It still finds its way to my stereo about once every two or three weeks. While I have changed radically since the day Mark and I first busted it from its sleeve and listened to it in my mother's living room, the recording still remains indelibly the same. There is still that brief hitch—a breath, or the end of sentence—before the guitar line begins in "I Will Dare."

My whole approach to listening to music has altered. Not only has the way by which I listen to music (compact discs and MP3s) changed, but my relationship to music has become incredibly more involved. Having spent several hundred hours in studio sessions, I can't listen to a record without picking apart its bones, reducing it to its bare tracks, wondering over how they got the drum sound, what vocal mic they used, how long it took them to nail that one intro. It feels stodgy compared to the near-osmotic way by which music would seep into my veins as a kid, uninhibited by the censoring functions of my logical brain. It's rare that I'll hear a song or record that grabs me the way it did when I was younger—and even then, the way it moves me has none of the mystery that went along with a discovery of a new band.

My moving away from Montana, in 1993, coincided with the rapid growth of the Internet, which, for secluded music fans, provided a wealth of easily accessible information on nearly every band in existence. Even though I bemoaned the fact that what I learned of the history of bands came via my uncle Paul through our telephone conversations, what was concealed from me only heightened the mythology that surrounded the music I was discovering.

*   *   *

And here I am now, in a band myself. It's my sixth band, including my turn as a member of the Babies. The studied impressions of Replacements, Hüsker Dü, Robyn Hitchcock, and Camper Van Beethoven songs that I was taught by various guitar teachers and mentors along the line eventually morphed into my own songs. And although I never quite grasped the finer nuances of guitar playing like my uncle predicted (to this day, I can't play a technical guitar solo to save my life), in most respects, my boyhood dream has come true.

In the spring of 2003, my band the Decemberists were on a nationwide tour supporting the reissue of our first record, *Castaways and Cutouts*. It was my first major

tour—previously I had only done short, coastal runs—
and we were playing in cities I had never visited. One
of those cities was Minneapolis. As we drove into the
city limits, we played Hüsker Dü and the Replacements
on the stereo. As we pulled off the interstate and began
weaving our way towards the club I stared out the tinted
window and watched the gray streets speed by, half
expecting to see Paul Westerberg and the rest of the
'Mats shuffling down the sidewalk. We parked the van
in front of the club, the 400 Bar, and walked in, shaking
our limbs free of stiffness. The interior of the club was
dirty and small and stunk of cigarette smoke and we
all began meandering about, examining the stage and
looking for the bar manager.

As I stood, dazed, in the middle of the club, I heard
Rachel, our drummer, say, "Come look at this!"

I walked over to where she was standing, pointing
at three framed pictures on the wall. Standing next
to her, I recognized the subjects of the photos as the
Replacements. Rachel and I stood in awe. Here was
Paul Westerberg, standing with Johnny Thunders on
stage; here was a photo of Bob Stinson, beer in hand,
laughing at something Tommy was saying; here, a picture of mop-topped Chris Mars, his mouth agape, his
drumsticks railing on his kit.

"They're all over the place," said Rachel, as we
turned to another wall. Framed concert notices, tickets,

and newspaper clippings covered the walls of the club, all in memorial to the Replacements, the drunken pride of Minneapolis. As we stood, looking at a picture of Paul Westerberg on stage at a small club while a similarly messy-haired man handed him a guitar, someone came up behind us.

"That's my brother," the voice said, pointing to the gentleman holding the guitar. "Their tour manager, Bill Sullivan."

It was the club owner—a tall man with glasses and a balding pate.

"Bobby used to come and drink here all the time," the man said. "His parents' house was just around the corner. Here, look." He lead us over to another wall, equally festooned with framed Replacements memorabilia. On the wall, there was a picture of the four band members, sitting on a roof top, mugging for the camera. It was obviously from the same roll that produced the cover for *Let It Be*. "That's the Stinsons' house," he said, before he was called away by the bartender to answer a phone call.

Rachel and I stayed for a moment, studying the photograph, mentally measuring it against the cover of the record, staring at the frozen, unchanging facial expressions of the four Replacements, and then walked off to the van to load in our gear. The street was dirty and the fenders of the van were flecked with mud. Most of the buildings surrounding the club were gray and dilapidated; the sidewalks were cracked and broken. It was May and the trees in the neighborhood were only then regaining their leaves, their growth stunted by yet another harsh, subzero winter and from where I stood, holding open the back door of our van, I could just begin to map the individual lives of the Replacements to these dirty, winding streets . . .

*　　*　　*

The year is 1978, and Paul Westerberg is hiding in the bushes. It's early April and the snow lies in patches at his feet. That which is not covered in snow is bathed in a deep layer of mud. He shifts his Converse'd size twelveses to a patch of dirt flecked-snow, grimacing at his mudspattered soles. He does not come from a wealthy family—his father is a Cadillac salesman—and he is being overly conscious about the condition of his new shoes. His attention is drawn quickly away, however, by the noise that has drawn him to this position in the first place. The melody is elusive and the playing is immeasurably sloppy, but he's now beginning to piece together what had drawn him to this shrubbery re-treat—it is unmistakably Yes. "Long Distance Run-around," in fact. He swats away an offending bow and stares at the house from which the music is emanating, pouring from the shaking windows like big rays of light. When he first stopped, he hadn't realized it was Yes. He assumed it was something much more edgy—he heard a myriad of influences in the music: a bit of Ramones, Talking Heads, New York Dolls. He was now shocked to find that it had been Yes all along. But it was Yes played with such a callow disregard for form and function that it ceased to carry any of the prog-snob trappings of the original. The music is all blaze and fury—the drumming is roughshod and spastic, on a constant brink of collapse; the bass is ugly and is obviously being played poorly through very cheap equipment; the guitar, however, is what is really grabbing young Paul, his feet teetering in mud in the bushes outside the house. It is gross and growling, tumbling through its arpeggios like an aerialist, sawing blindly at Yes' studied maneuvers until it is only the impression that remains. Paul is dumbfounded. His right foot slips and he falls backwards into a large patch of mud, covering the back of his Levis.

The bass player is twelve years old. His hair is a shaggy, sandy blond that falls across his boyish face. His name is Tommy and his brother, Bobby, is the guitar player in the band. They're called Dogbreath. Lanky Chris, with his curly, moppish hair spilling over his shoulders, is their drummer. They play covers of the hard rock songs that are currently popular on the radio stations of Minneapolis. They play AC/DC, Ted Nugent, Black Sabbath. When Paul asks them if they're familiar with the bands that he distinctly heard in their sloppy covers, they look dumbfounded. They all come from decidedly working class families; Bobby is a high school drop out. He is the quintessential older brother to Tommy: he is condescending and churlish, but in the end sweetly protective. Bobby is the one responsible for thrusting the bass guitar responsibilities upon Tommy. He's afraid that he'll end up like their parents—or worse, like himself. Bobby drinks too much, smokes too much pot, lives with his parents and works as a pizza cook. Teaching his little brother Motorhead songs is a way of negating his current downward spiral, hoping that this four string piece of wood and electronics will somehow give Tommy a chance to do something that seems out of Bobby's grasp.

Paul is now standing in the middle of the Stinsons' basement. Mrs. Stinson's footsteps clatter above the floor ducts above his head. He is trying to teach Dogbreath a new song, a song from one of his cherished LPs. It is "Personality Crisis," by the New York Dolls. The band appear nonplussed. Regardless of what their playing style might suggest, it becomes obvious that they are not fond of punk rock. Drummer Chris keeps mixing up the beats, Bobby gets bored of the two-chord swagger and begins haphazardly soloing over the verses.

Tommy is the only one paying rapt attention. He is staring at Paul's fretboard intently, watching each chord shift and trying to parlay the information to his own stunted fingers. Paul, against his better judgment, has to stop the song continually to correct his bandmates. He can scarcely believe that this is the same group he has spent so many hours listening to in secret, his shoes muddy to the gunwales. Bobby is the first to give up and instead launches into a sped-up version of "Iron Man." Paul shrugs and follows along.

Their first show is in a church basement. Tommy has broken his arm, and the band is forced to enjoy its debut performance with only half of its rhythm section. At Paul's urging, they've changed their name from Dogbreath—the name didn't strike him as being particularly memorable—to the Impediments. They immediately run into a problem, however: the promoter doesn't like the anti-handicapped implications of their new name, says it isn't very Presbyterian. And this being a Presbyterian church and all. On the spot, they pick The Replacements. They're each of them shaking with nervousness. Bobby, with a shake of his head, indicates he has something in his van that might alleviate their fears. They drink rum and Cokes in the back of his van; they pop Vicodin and head back into the church. They play the show to a smattering of friends, church functionaries, and family members. The applause at the end of the set is sparse but heartfelt and the three non-injured Replacements meet out by Paul's car after the show for cigarettes and beer. They crack jokes and talk about the show they've just played, each one secretly imagining himself backstage at 1st Avenue, barking with professional nonchalance about their performance. They go to a pool hall and get drunk and shoot pool.

*   *   *

They're playing at the 7th Avenue Entry downtown for two dollars. Peter Jesperson, their manager, has just pressed up 100 copies of their new EP, "Stink." Their friends Hüsker Dü are headlining the show. The air in the dark club is moist with perspiration—the floor is a sea of leather jackets and shiny bald heads, all violently oscillating around a central point on the floor. Hüsker Dü is playing now and Paul is drinking his sixth whiskey and coke of the evening. Tommy is standing by the pinball machine, quietly waiting his turn as a heavy set punker slams at the paddles. The bouncer is watching the fourteen year old intently, dismayed that he's been given this extra responsibility. Bobby and Chris are nowhere to be found. Paul slams back his whiskey and coke and goes charging headlong onto the dance floor, his flannel, jeans, and sneakers a strange departure from the wardrobe *de rigeur* in the pit tonight. He elbows someone in the jaw, only to get knocked on the ground by an errant shoulder. A hand appears out of the pit's swirling human fog, offering assistance. Paul spits blood on the floor and angrily kicks himself to a stand.

*   *   *

They're into their third case of Primo beer. Its early evening at the Stinson house; they're in the basement, recording into Mr. Stinson's Sony boombox. They've been joking about how they're going to record their whole next record on it, but now that it's later and they're into their third case of Primo beer, they're pretty serious about it. They're making up songs as they go along—Bobby and Paul have acoustic guitars (Bobby's missing his B string), Tommy's playing his bass through a practice amp, and Chris is playing brushes on his snare. They play "Radio Free Europe" to the tune of Elvis Costello's "Radio Radio," and Paul laughs through the second verse. They are now playing a country tune, one that Paul has actually taken the time to think up words to. Tommy is laughing over the words, which seem to sum up the last several years of the band— relentless, underpaying tours; callous, irresponsible label owners; steady inebriation. "We're gettin' nowhere / Quick as we know how / We're gettin' nowhere . . . " Here Paul stumbles, suddenly realizing he had messed up the words, thus breaking up the rhyme. He slurs, "What do we do now?" He decides a guitar solo would be the only thing to save the song from its own demise. He shouts "Take it, Scotty!" to Bob, who is just at that point reaching for his can of beer. Surprised by this sudden call to action, Bob leaps back to his guitar, knocking over a pile of empty beer cans in the process. The song, like the pile of empties, falls sputtering to an end and Tommy bursts into laughter. "What're the chords to that one part again?" he shouts as each Replacement reaches for another beer. "Fucked 'em up," slurs Paul, half-lidded. He cracks a rye smile. The song will be the closing track of their third album.

*   *   *

That record, *Hootenanny*, has been named the best album of 1983 by the *New York Times*. The band had only been to New York a few times—their collective memory of the city amounts to a few blurry nights at CBGB's—but they're all a little bowled over by the implications of the notice. Except for Bobby, who's standing in the Twin/Tone offices with his hands folded across his chest. They've just gotten off a tour with R.E.M., a band enjoying a seemingly unbridled rise to fame within the college circuit, and the band's guitar player, Pete Buck, wants to do some work with them in the studio. Again, Bobby has mixed feelings about this. In his opinion, they've moved farther away from the punk trash of their inception; the songs that Paul is bringing to practice are sounding more and more like *pop*.

"You just want us to keep playing 'War Pigs' in your parents basement, don't you?" yells Paul, bothered by Bobby's attitude.

Bob sneers. "Yes," he says.

*   *   *

"Ow . . . fuck!" shouts Tommy, jerking his hand back from the window pane, "I think I got a sliver." He studies his thumb for a moment, searching for the offending wound. Bobby pushes past him, pries open the window and, all the while carrying a can of beer in one hand, manages to navigate his body through the open window and out onto the roof. He dusts off his jeans and looks out over the neighborhood. It's his parents' house, the house he's been living in his whole life, and the landscape that rolls out before him is intimately familiar.

Paul sticks his head out. "This gonna work?" says Paul.

"Oh yeah," Bobby replies. He extends a hand to Paul.

"Fuck that," Paul says, "I don't need your goddamn help." He pushes himself out the window on to the roof.

He does not manage the feat as gracefully as Bobby; the beer he is carrying empties on to the roof shingles and he curses. "Hey Tommy!" he shouts back into the house, "Make sure to bring me another beer." A second's pause. "Just bring the whole case."

Tommy tosses the half-rack of Primo out on to the roof, like a climber stowing his gear before making a descent, and clambers out of the window, carefully protecting his wounded thumb. He's bandaged it now, but a little blood is seeping through the white tape. Chris and the photographer follow last, each taking a moment to take in the view before reaching into the case of beer for another can. The pitch of the roof is steep, and they all move about precariously. Chris almost falls while opening his can of beer; Tommy shouts at the next door neighbor kid for letting his dog shit in their yard.

Finally, they all settle into their places, sitting. The photographer edges backwards on the roof, carefully watching how far he can go. The band jokes with him; tells him just to go a little bit farther—just a bit farther. Finally, he finds a comfortable place and aims the camera at the four lanky men on the rooftop. Tommy reaches up and wipes some sleep from his eye as the camera clicks.

*   *   *

Also available in the series